LOOKING BACK AT
POPULAR
ENTERTAINMENT
1901·1939

Marie Lloyd

LOOKING BACK AT
POPULAR ENTERTAINMENT
1901 · 1939

Ann Purser

EP Publishing Limited 1978

Copyright © Ann Purser, 1978

This edition first published 1978
by EP Publishing Limited
East Ardsley, Wakefield, West Yorkshire,
England

ISBN: 0 7158 1205 X

Please address all enquiries to:
EP Publishing Limited (address as above)

Printed by G. Beard & Son Ltd,
Brighton, Sussex

Contents

Heydays on the Halls

Imagine that it's a Saturday night in 1901, and you live in a narrow red-brick house with five brothers and three sisters and your Gran, in the East End of London, say Hoxton or Bethnal Green, and your Mum and Dad are looking forward to their favourite evening's entertainment. Can you guess what it is? It's not the latest spectacular on television, nor a James Bond film at the local cinema. It's not a Saturday night radio play, nor a session with the stereo music centre. In 1901 none of these were yet available.

Well, what else is there? Perhaps you haven't guessed, because the answer doesn't really exist any more. But at the end of the last century and the beginning of this one, Music Hall was the most flourishing and popular entertainment for vast numbers of people. You will see from the way it grew, that it was enjoyed mostly by working people, and it was not always thought respectable enough for men to take their wives. Its songs were the pop songs of the day, spread around by sales of song sheets, and errand boys' whistling. There were dozens of errand boys in every town in those days, bicycling lads who delivered groceries, meat and vegetables, and generally ran errands for very small wages.

Music Hall stars were the pop stars of their day. Coming mostly from the working people, they were often vulgar, brash, colourful and very good at their job of keeping an extremely difficult audience amused. All over the country thousands of people flocked to see their favourites, knew the songs by heart, imitated the way the stars dressed, and repeated their catch-words.

Music Hall is generally traced back through the Pleasure Gardens created in the cities to the Musick Rooms of Elizabeth I's reign. For instance, at Sadler's Wells in the 1830s a boy could take his girlfriend through the twinkling lighted trees to a tent, where for three hours they could watch comedy, ballet, tightrope walking, a strong man, balancing tricks, mime; and after all that, an operetta as well!

Then in the nineteenth century there were the Penny Gaffs and Cider Cellars. These were dark and dismal places where the very poor went to be amused by fairly low-standard performances, and the better-off went to disapprove of them. The Penny Gaff was usually in a converted shop or stable, it was dimly lit by candles, and the audience sat on uncomfortable benches at—as you might guess—the price of an old penny (worth less than $\frac{1}{2}$p today) each. For two old pence you could reserve yourself a seat, as they were very crowded and popular. Living conditions in the East End of London were very bad; people lived in squalid, overcrowded and smelly houses built on dust heaps. Murder and violence were common, and the Penny Gaff jokes and songs were about the misfortunes of the East End people. It was an hour-long show, which didn't begin until enough people had arrived, and it was a great attraction for thieves, pickpockets and other criminals.

This "bad" character of the Penny Gaffs rubbed off on the Music Hall, and for many years Music Halls were not considered a respectable place for a family outing.

As well as the Penny Gaffs, there were the Song and Supper Rooms of the mid-nineteenth century. These were for the better-off gentlemen (their ladies watched through grilles), and they had a Chairman who faced the audience and announced the acts. The performers were much more polished and respectable, and the most famous supper room, Evans in Covent Garden, was visited by Edward VII when he was Prince of Wales.

The names of the artists were known to enthusiastic audiences. One called W. G. Ross sang a favourite but gloomy song about Sam Hall, a chimney sweep about to be hanged for murder:

Evans Supper Room in the mid-nineteenth century

The song cover for one of Marie Lloyd's well-known songs

My name is Sam Hall, Chimney Sweep,
My name it is Sam Hall,
I robs both great and small,
But they makes me pay for all—
Damn their eyes!

Music Rooms and Harmonic Halls were attached to pubs like the Eagle (remember "Pop goes the Weasel"?—"Up and down the City Road, in and out The Eagle"). The first proper Music Hall, which grew out of all these different places of entertainment, is said to have been at the Canterbury Arms in Lambeth, south of the river in London, started by its proprietor, Charles Morton, who was called the Grand Old Man of Music Hall.

Lots of Music Halls were opened after the Canterbury, like Gatti's Music Hall where your father is taking your mother tonight, dressed in her best taffeta, to hear Marie Lloyd sing "The Boy I Love is Up in The Gallery" and "Then You Wink the Other Eye". You can see the song cover for "Then You Wink the Other Eye" on the previous page. The really famous Music Hall stars, once they'd reached the top, played in pantomime at the "straight" theatres like the Drury Lane and also gave recitals for the rich in their own drawing-rooms. On this page you can see Albert Chevalier, a Music Hall star, performing one of his coster songs. A Coster was an East End trader in vegetables and food, who carried his wares about on a long barrow. You may have seen the Pearly Kings and Queens, with shiny pearl buttons sewn in beautiful patterns on their suits and hats; they were modelled on the original Costermongers of London.

Although they were always thought less respectable than what is called the "legitimate" theatre, where plays and opera were performed, the Halls themselves became very grand. There were fountains, and palm trees in tubs in the foyer, chandeliers of bright lights, and elegant decorations inside the Hall. The stage had elaborately draped curtains, and costumes were glamorous. The Promenade of earlier days (where girls walked up and down) had gone, and the audience now sat respectfully in rows, no longer in

Albert Chevalier performing one of his coster songs

groups around tables, chattering, drinking and hardly attending to the stage.

Marie Lloyd—perhaps one of the most famous of Music Hall artists—started performing at fifteen at the Grecian Saloon where her father was a waiter. She was renowned for her neatness and elegance. She had golden hair, big blue eyes and wore beautiful dresses made by her mother and aunt. One of her favourites was in white satin embroidered with gold and silver threads, wild blush roses, sequins, spangles and tiny tinted shells. She carried a long cane studded with diamanté and wore a tiny hat tilted over one eye. And yet, although she looked so elegant, her favourite supper was bread and dripping, with the gravy from the bottom of the basin! Music Hall was for the working people, and its artists were working class too.

Twelve years after your imaginary evening in Hoxton, the Music Hall was at last made truly respectable by a Royal Command Performance for King George V and Queen

Here you can see the audience at the last performance at the Canterbury Music Hall in May, 1912

Mary—and many people say that was the end of it! The secret of the Music Hall's long popularity was its down-to-earth, sometimes rudely jolly character. And naturally the acts cannot be so rude when Kings and Queens are in the audience.

But in the heyday of the Music Hall, which most people agree to have been from about 1890 to 1912, its stars shone very brightly indeed.

That evening in 1901 your parents might well have seen some other famous performers on the same bill at Gatti's Music Hall. The one I would most like to have seen was "Little Tich" (when you call your rather small friend "Tich", that's where the name came from). Little Tich's best-known turn was the "Big Boot Dance". His real name was Harry Relph, he was small and quick-moving, and he had six fingers on each hand. He very much disliked this oddity and would usually wear gloves. His other oddity was chosen for his act and these were his fantastically long boots—several feet long. As he was himself only four feet and a few inches tall, he must have looked very strange and L-shaped on the stage.

He danced in these boots, performed comic sketches with his hat and stick, and would lean right over the orchestra pit (just in front of the stage) at a dangerous angle, supported by his elongated toes.

In private life, Little Tich was a serious and studious person, but in the Music Hall, he was always accompanied by quick lively tunes and he was a great favourite. There were some people who did not like his act, because he seemed to be asking his audience to laugh at his deformity—much as the tiny, reedy-voiced Charlie Drake does today—but most of the Music Hall audiences had no such qualms, and loved Little Tich in pantomime as well as in the Halls. He was even awarded the Legion d'Honneur in France, rather like the MBE being awarded to the Beatles or Mike Yarwood in this country.

Another kind of act which would perhaps not be so well received today, but which was a great success then, was the Nigger Minstrel Troupe, with names like Haverley's Minstrels

Little Tich and his "Big Boots"

and the Mohawks. These were white performers "blacked up", that is, made up to look like Negroes. They came originally from America and would sing in public halls for family entertainment; they sang such songs as "Jeannie with the Light Brown Hair", "Heap Pretty Flowers on my Grave", "Kiss Me Mother 'ere I Die", "Close the Shutter, Willie's Dead". They seemed to have had a taste for the gloomy and morbid!

Some of their performers moved into the Music Halls as solo acts. Eugene Stratton was known as "The Idol of the Halls" and as well as singing famous songs like "Lily of Laguna" (ask your grandfather—he'll know that one), he did a beautiful soft shoe shuffle. This kind of dancing has now disappeared, but it was very graceful, light and airy to watch. The dancer had soft shoes on, which "stroked" the stage in rhythmic patterns, and all his limbs were loose and relaxed.

One Nigger Minstrel who could still be seen on the stage up till fairly recently, was G. H. Elliott, The Chocolate Coloured Coon; he sang a sentimental song to his plump attractive wife Lindy-Lou and his singing voice would be an imitation of a deep Negro bass. People did laugh at the comic antics of the Nigger Minstrels, as well as appreciating their songs, but no more than they laughed at comics who pretended to be simple lads from out of town, like George Formby Senior (father of the ukelele-playing George Formby whom you see sometimes in old films), who had worked up an act called "Little Willie from Lancashire".

Music Hall audiences on the whole came into the warmth and gaiety of the theatre atmosphere from a tough, rough life in the poor districts of London, and they were not so sensitive about hurt feelings, and what was "suitable" for a good laugh. They were not backward in showing what they thought of an act either! Performers dreaded "the bird"; raucous shouts of "Shut up! Chuck him out! Shut yer face, dear, I can see yer Christmas dinner!" The "scarlet bird" was worse, for the audience would rise and bellow furiously until the curtain came down.

Who else was on the bill that night in 1901? Well, it might have been Vesta Tilley or Hetty King. Both ladies impersonated men and they were very popular.

Vesta Tilley was an elegant young woman, who married well and became Lady de Frece. She used to sing the famous "I'm Burlington Bertie, I rise at ten-thirty, and toddle along to the Strand" (the Strand was a street in London). Another male impersonator in the Halls, Ella Shields, had a different version of this song, which showed clearly how in those days you were either very rich or very poor, and if you had fallen out of luck, life could be hard. Ella's sad version went "I'm Bert . . . p'raps you've heard of me, Bert . . . you've had word of me, jogging along, hearty and strong, living on plates of fresh air." (Ella Shields had come from

Vesta Tilley as Burlington Bertie

13

America as a "Coon Shouter". This was a white performer who sang Negro songs in ragtime style; you'll read more about ragtime later.)

There were dozens of other Music Hall stars, and anyone you can find who remembers those days will have his own favourite— perhaps the great Charlie Chaplin, with flat feet, walking stick, sad expression and battered hat, who became the most famous film star of all, but started on the stage of the Music Hall, and was a member of the famous Fred Karno's Companies. Perhaps it would be Dan Leno, who began his stage life at three years old at a Music Hall called the Cosmotheka, and was billed as "Little George, the Infant Wonder, Contortionist and Posturer". He became so famous that King Edward VII was one of his fans, and Leno was known as "The King's Jester".

Another child wonder was Wee Georgie Wood, whose mother was a ferocious woman who was determined her son should succeed, and who made him work far too hard. You would find his act a bit strange now. He had a "Nursery at Bedtime" sketch and danced with a golliwog who was played by Arthur Stanley Jefferson, otherwise Stan Laurel of the Laurel and Hardy comic team, who still make us laugh when their films are shown on television today.

The list of stars could be very long, and you might wonder how they all made a living. But remember again that in the heyday of the Music Hall there was no television, no cinema, no radio, and no gramophone to speak of. It was the only place for the mass of the people to go to be entertained. Richer people had other ways of enjoying themselves, as you will see, but Music Hall was the biggest, noisiest, most colourful and most popular way of having a night out.

There were, for example, at the turn of the century, more than five hundred Music Halls in Central London alone. And every biggish provincial town had its Music Hall too, where the famous stars would visit on tour. It might be fun to see if you can find out where your nearest Music Hall was. Sometimes the buildings are still standing and being used for all sorts of other purposes.

The stars did, in fact, do very well at the height of their popularity. Vesta Tilley (who at her farewell performance took seventeen curtain calls and had a ladder of fame made of violets stretching from floor to ceiling on the stage behind her) was earning £350 a week in the 1900s and Albert Chevalier (the Coster singer) could ask for £450 a week when he went round the country on tour. If you consider that this would be now worth about seven times as much, the top performers were certainly well paid!

When, in 1907, the important stars formed themselves into one big "union", the National Alliance of Music Hall Artists, they were powerful enough to call a strike to help the less successful Music Hall performers. The strikers won. These stars were much-loved, and knew well their popularity with the people. When Marie Lloyd died, pubs were draped in black, and about 100,000 people watched her funeral. The procession had twelve cars smothered in flowers, there was a huge model of a stage with red roses, hundreds of wreaths, and on top of the hearse, Marie's famous diamanté-studded cane. Marie Lloyd had paid nightly for one hundred and fifty beds for the down-and-outs of London, and she was always very generous to anyone who asked for help. She collapsed on stage and when she died only a few hours later, her loyal audiences from working-class London were heart-broken.

Music Hall was—as its name says plainly— a musical entertainment, and some of its greatest songs are still around. Lottie Collins used to sing "Ta-ra-ra Boom-de-ay" with great gusto, and not so long ago children in school were still singing their version: "Ta-ra-ra Boom-de-ay, we're breaking up today, that's why we're very gay, ta-ra-ra boom-de-ay."

You can still find piano music for the old songs. Nowadays they tend to be collector's items, but you might be lucky enough to come across some, such as the following, which was sung by Marie Lloyd:

We went gatherin' Carslips (Cowslips)
Moo-cow came to me,
Wagged 'is apparatus,
And I said unto he,
Rumptiddley-umptiddley-umptiddley-ay,
Our little lot so gay,
We won't care what we do or what we say

Or you might find Harry Champion's song:

When I was a nipper only six months old,
My mother and my father too,
They didn't know what to feed me on,
They were both in a dreadful stew;
They thought of tripe, they thought of steak,
Or a little bit of old cods roe,
I said "Pop round to the old cook-shop,
I know what'll make me grow

"Boiled beef and carrots,
Boiled beef and carrots,
That's the stuff for your Derby-kel,
Makes you fat and keeps you well—

Don't live like vegetarians,
On food they give to parrots,
From morn to night blow out your kite,
On boiled beef and carrots."

("Derby-kel" was cockney rhyming slang for belly.)

Your mother and father's night out is coming to an end—but after the live acts a white screen might be lowered and a flickering, silent, black and white moving picture would be shown. This was often a way of getting the audience out of the Hall. They were warm, boozy and comfortable, and quite happy to stay awhile. As the first shadowy, indistinct moving pictures were not a great attraction to an audience in this cheery mood, they might mutter and grumble in the darkened Music Hall, and leave for home. But the Bioscope, or early cinema, had arrived, and as you will discover, it was the beginning of the end for Music Hall.

Stage, Screen and the Grizzly Bear Rag

What else could you do in the early 1900s besides going to the Music Hall? As we have said, Music Hall was a place where thousands of working people went to enjoy themselves. What about the richer people?

Well, in the towns there was the theatre. Not the Music Hall theatre, but "straight" entertainment on stage. There was musical comedy and revue, and there were serious plays, not only by classical writers like Shakespeare but by more modern writers like Pinero, a marvellous story-teller, and Oscar Wilde, whose witty and elegant plays like *The Importance of Being Earnest* still give us a great deal of pleasure today.

John Galsworthy wrote plays such as *Strife* and *Justice*, which were a new kind of drama dealing with problems of everyday life, and not at all the escape into never-never land which many of the musical comedies and revues were. George Bernard Shaw, too, was a great writer who wrote about problems of the day, slums, war and religion, and how people actually felt and what they worried about.

One of the most popular entertainments which your parents would have liked if they were reasonably well off and living in a respectable suburb of London such as Wimbledon, would be a visit to a musical comedy at the New Gaiety Theatre in Aldwych.

You dressed up to go to the Gaiety. You arrived in a brougham (a horse-drawn carriage) and if you were a lady you carried a fan of waving feathers, and had an elaborate and beautiful dress, with jewels in your hair, round your neck and on your fingers. If you were a man, you wore a smart, tailored black evening suit, a stiff white shirt, a top hat and a cloak.

Part of the pleasure of such an outing was dressing up for the evening, and you would more than likely have had a maid to help you get ready.

The Gaiety Theatre had been a famous home of glamorous shows, lovely girls and light, catchy tunes for many years (and before that, it had housed "burlesque", a kind of theatre which mocked straight plays and got laughs by being very exaggerated and theatrical). The most famous manager of the Gaiety was George Edwardes and during his "reign" there, it was the centre of gay and sparkling life in London.

The stars of these Gaiety shows were worshipped by all the theatregoers, who would wait outside the theatre after the performance, often as late as eleven o'clock, when the girls would walk like queens down an avenue of "fans". But no-one asked for an autograph! That wasn't thought at all suitable then, and if you wanted a star's signature you had to write in to the theatre.

The Gaiety Girls were the chorus line, and all were plump, tall and handsome. It didn't much matter if they couldn't sing or dance too well, their job was to look elegant and beautiful. These girls were much sought after by the men-about-town, called "mashers", and each of the Big Eight (the leading line of

The Gaiety Girls

girls) had a whole string of admirers who would wait for them after the show and take them out to supper in the smartest restaurants in town, like Romano's, the Café Royal and Oddenino's. One of these girls, Ada Reeve, remembered long afterwards being presented with a bunch of orchids by her admirer before being taken off to a light supper of pâté, plover's eggs, roast chicken and, of course, champagne. Some mashers who were very keen on a particular Gaiety Girl would go ten or twelve times to the same show, just to glimpse their favourites in the chorus line, and to gaze at her through opera-glasses. Occasionally one of the girls married her aristocratic admirer, and many of the other girls dreamed of doing the same.

The scenery and costumes on stage were very grand and cost a lot of money. One show, *The Circus Girl*, had a circus scene with a real horse coming on stage. They had trouble with this horse, however, as it had been employed as an omnibus horse (there were no motor buses then) for most of its working life and the only thing which would induce it to move was the stage-manager shouting a long list of bus stops—Charing Cross, Strand, Bank, Piccadilly. Then he would bang a door, shout, "Right behind!", and the horse would obediently move forward onto the stage, with the star of the show riding on top.

Stars like Marie Tempest (her behaviour was as tempestuous as her name), Gertie Millar and Gabrielle Ray, who created a sensation by appearing on stage in 1903 in pink silk pyjamas, appeared in musical comedies like *The Country Girl*, *The Merry Widow*, or *The Chocolate Soldier*, and the theatre-going public loved them. They led lives as glamorous as their stage appearances, going to fancy dress balls at midnight at Covent Garden Theatre (Covent Garden is where the famous vegetable market in London used to be), and then travelling home in cabs which charged ten times the normal fare. There were days in the country spent idyllically lolling in a punt, while a handsome young man propelled them up and down the Thames; there were picnics and luscious meals at the famous Skindles Hotel at Maidenhead, and back to supper at the Star and Garter at Richmond, where the terraces and gardens were lit by fairy lights.

It was a golden, glittering life. The Big Eight girls were paid £15 a week, which was a lot of money then, and the solid, secure English middle and upper classes loved it all. They sang the songs from the shows from sheet music which they played on their parlour pianos. (200,000 copies of "The Merry Widow Waltz" were sold between 1907 and 1909.) They wore huge Merry Widow hats; and in America, where the same show had a terrific success, they had Merry Widow chocolates, cigars and even Merry Widow corsets!

Then at Christmas, of course, there was—yes, pantomime. The Christmas pantomimes in the early 1900s were jolly and spectacular just as they are now. But there were no references to television shows, and the stars of pantomime came from Music Hall, and the songs too. There would be the stories that we know today such as *Cinderella*, *Mother Goose*, *Jack and the Beanstalk* and *Babes in the Wood*. Further back in the nineteenth century, pantomime had sprung from the traditional story of Harlequin and Columbine, the Clown and Pantaloon, but by our century, this had just about disappeared from pantomime shows, and now there was a romantic heroine and a principal boy, played by a girl. The comic Dames (played by men, the most famous being Dan Leno, mentioned in the last chapter, from Music Hall), and the usual comedy acts and songs.

Aladdin, produced in a very "Chinese" style, had this tinkling chorus to open the show:

Scene from "The Merry Widow" (taken at a performance in 1907)

Dan Leno as Mother Goose at the Drury Lane Theatre, London, in 1904

Citizens of Peking,
Velly honest we,
Cally on our bus'less,
Likee Littee bee,
Makee muchee chop-chop,
Workee velly good,
Gettee biggee bonus,
Ev'lybody should!
Happy China mannee
While he workee sing,
Ching-a-ring-a-ring ching,
Ching-ching-ching!

It all sounds very like the pantomime of today, but if you look at the picture of the chorus line on the next page, you will see that there were differences!

The villain was very villainous, of course, and children would shriek and scream at his entrance. Abanazar (played by an actor called Robert Hale) in Aladdin at the Drury Lane Theatre in 1917, had the following lines which raised a shiver as well as a laugh:

When I shewed in my hey-day, the
    Vanishing Lady,
(Great Scott! What a peach! What a gem!)
All the husbands, you see, brought their
    wives round to me,
Just to ask me if I'd vanish them!

"Comic interludes" were popular in pantomime, much as they are today, with silly jokes and acts which didn't have much to do with the actual story.

In Robinson Crusoe, when Little Tich played Man Friday, this comic exchange had them rolling in the aisles:

Crusoe: You speak English?
Man Friday: Yes! A missionary taught it
             me, I guess.
Crusoe: He must have geen a good
             man!
Friday: Yes, he *was*!
             I nebber knew a better.
Crusoe: Why?
Friday: Becos . . .
             After he'd taught me
             everything he knew, I ate
             him! Nice man!

As nowadays, there was a really Grand Finale, and the principal boy had a farewell speech to make. An odd theatrical superstition was that the very last two lines must never be spoken until the first night of the pantomime. To speak them at rehearsals would bring terribly bad luck.

Well, that was Christmas, but what else was there to go and see in the early 1900s? As well as serious plays about modern life by the writers we have mentioned, there was something called melodrama. This meant exciting plays with exaggerated plots, full of murder, sobbing maidens, and wicked stepfathers or uncles. The virtuous girl was nearly always

A scene from the pantomime, "Cinderella"

poor and her wicked seducer who ruined her life was nearly always rich and aristocratic. He certainly never thought of marrying her! *Maria Marten; or the Murder in the Red Barn* was one of the best known of these melodramas.

The most famous actor ever, some say, was Henry Irving, who during the 1880s and 1890s had become a legend, and remained so long after his death in 1905. He kept a high standard of melodrama going, as well as playing in productions of Shakespeare. Irving was an actor/manager, and this particular combination of job—managing a theatre, producing its plays and acting in them—was very popular during those years. One of his most famous leading ladies was Ellen Terry, who celebrated 50 years as an actress in 1906.

You may be beginning to think that all popular entertainment went on in London, and nowhere else. But of course this is not true.

Before the 1900s, there had been theatres in many towns and cities all over the country, with their own Music Halls, pantomimes and plays performed by stock companies. These were groups of actors and stage hands who belonged to one theatre or several in the same area. When travel by train became so much easier and cheaper towards the end of the nineteenth century, the touring companies arrived with their versions of the latest London shows, and stole much of the popularity of the stock companies.

Nowadays, when actors can play any part at all with good make-up and camera tricks, it is rather odd to think that in those days each member of the stock company had his favourite sort of part, which he was especially good at, the Old Man, the Old Woman, the Heavy Father, the Juvenile Lead (the chief young part) and the Low Comedian, whilst the

Walking-on Lady or Gentleman had small, less important parts. Some of these old-fashioned descriptions are still used in the theatre today.

By 1901, however, cheap travel also meant that audiences could travel to the bigger, more lavish theatres, and many of the smaller ones were no longer operating. Then, in 1908, a lady who was already very well-known in the theatre, Miss Horniman, bought the Gaiety Theatre in Manchester. There she set up a company of the type you may know about already: a Repertory Theatre. "Repertory" just meant that the company of actors who stayed with the same theatre, put on a different play every week or fortnight, or sometimes each night, and the local people had an opportunity to go regularly to the theatre to be entertained by something new. They got to know their favourite actors and actresses, of course, and it was a very friendly, local occasion, though grand people in London rather looked down on "Rep" as an amateur affair. Glasgow followed with its own Repertory Theatre, and then Liverpool, and then many more opened all over the country. Repertory theatres were, and still are, very good places for new young actors to make a start.

The great Exhibitions of the early 1900s were not exactly theatres but certainly great entertainment, and were produced at White City and Earls Court. Just imagine you'd never seen a Western or a gangster film, or never seen exciting scenes on a grand scale, and then imagine you are being taken on a train (in itself a very exciting event) to see an Exhibition at Earls Court. These exhibitions were really to encourage trade abroad, and so there would be stands with goods from other countries on display, and plenty of other entertainment besides.

W. Macqueen Pope, who has written many books about the theatre, describes being taken as a boy to such an Exhibition at Earls Court. The year was 1899, just before the years of this book, but it is a very good description of a typical exhibition of those years. This exhibition was mainly about South Africa, the

magic land of gold mines, where many Englishmen were making a lot of money, and the native warrior tribes like the Matabele were fierce and warlike. The Boer War between the English and the original Dutch settlers in South Africa was still being fought in that year, so battles and massacres were very much in people's minds.

In the Exhibition, there were fabulous gold exhibits. There were bars and nuggets of gold from Witwatersrand, and fountains of mercury or quicksilver, which balanced flat irons on top of the silvery streams to show its miraculous properties. There were theatres, promenades, restaurants, and commercial exhibits of all sorts of inventions and manufactured goods of the time.

All this was free, except for the theatres and restaurants, of course, but beyond this was the entertainment. Here there was a rifle range, photo caricatures, an electro-phone, baby incubators, switchback railway, the Bioscope, the Great Wheel and a water chute.

Are you still imagining you are that child come up from the country? What bliss all this must be! Your legs may be aching, but you are anxious not to miss a single thing in this fantastic Exhibition before you go back to your village, where the most exciting events you can usually look forward to are the church or chapel concerts, or travelling shows with their makeshift melodramas.

You haven't seen everything at the Exhibition yet! At its Empress Theatre, a great spectacular has been arranged: two hundred Matabele warriors living in a specially constructed Kaffir Kraal (the South African natives were called Kaffirs), and you can pay 6d (this would be worth $2\frac{1}{2}$p in today's money) to go and stare at them. The programme for the Exhibition describes these warriors as "simple", "childlike" and "amusing", and says "They will provide endless sources of entertainment to the observant stranger." What do you think of that? It was a pretty horrible way of looking at a people who had their own civilisation and were as intelligent as you or I, or that boy seventy-odd years ago. But this is how people then considered the

The Franco-British Exhibition at the White City, London, in 1908

coloured natives, and they didn't mean to be unkind; they thought of themselves as "parents" or "protectors" and thought of the Matabele as untaught children.

The "great spectacular" used these native warriors in fearsome battles, ambushes and escapes, all on the Empress stage. They had real elephants, horses and guns, and the heroine always found herself in terrible danger with no-one to turn to for help. Of course, the soldiers won in the end, the heroine was rescued, and the audience went out of the theatre completely satisfied with the excitement and drama of it all. The bars were open all day, teas were served in the interval, and the boy from the country never forgot a visit to the Exhibition, not for the rest of his life.

Have we forgotten something which flickered at a sideshow at the Exhibition? What was it that ended the evening at the Music Hall attended by your mother and father in 1901?—the Bioscope, of course. And the Bioscope was moving pictures, which is exactly what the word kinema means. There was no sound track at this time, and so the movies were silent. The first few minutes of film, which hurried audiences out of the Music Hall, and which could be seen briefly at Earls Court, were the beginning of a new type of entertainment.

The very first public performance of the moving pictures was given by two Frenchmen, the brothers Lumière, who had brought their apparatus from France, and who arranged to give demonstrations of this marvellous new contraption at the Regent Street Polytechnic in London. Edison, the American who had invented the mechanism for moving pictures for home use, had never thought of them as public entertainment.

Of course, people had seen still slides projected on screens before, at the magic lantern shows which used to be given at home, in church halls and in parish rooms. But moving pictures were something tremendously exciting. Favourite subjects for these early films were street scenes with horse-drawn omnibuses moving along and people walking past shops. Most dramatic, and even frightening, were films of trains entering or leaving a station. With a camera placed at the right angle, the effect of an approaching train was so realistic that an audience in Paris had been reduced to absolute panic.

"Fancy being scared of a film!" you might say, but imagine yourself back again in time. You've never seen a film, either on television or in the cinema, and you are sitting in near darkness having no idea what to expect. Many older people have memories of being taken out of the kinema screaming with fright.

One elderly lady remembers, "We used to have weekly shows in the Co-op Hall. A screen was lowered and the film projected on to it. We used to say, 'Are you goin' in the plushies this week?'" The plushies were comfortable seats at the back and cost a few more pence than the hard benches at the front. "I only went because the other children went," she says, "I was scared stiff of this serial —an instalment every week—called *The Hand on the Wire* and this horrible hand came creeping round the door . . .", and the elderly lady shivered with the clear memory she had of her first visits to the moving pictures.

The Lumières themselves thought that the bioscope was only a showman's novelty, and that it wouldn't last. It appealed mostly to the poorer people, since it was very cheap—it only cost 1d in some places, and it was especially attractive to children who had nowhere warm to go, and who spent their days on the streets. The warm darkness was a haven, with the excitement of moving pictures of short comedies, early trick films, and trains and omnibuses, which were very popular.

In 1904, Cecil Hepworth made the first film with a real story to it; the film was called *Rescued by Rover*, and it cost the enormous sum of £7-13s-9d to make! It was the story of a dog finding a baby stolen from a pram by a beggar-woman, and it was the first in a long line of such melodramatic films. (You can see a scene from the film on page 25.)

In Hollywood, America, around 1910, two young men called Jesse Lasky and Cecil B. de Mille were getting together to make a "flic-

An early cinema projector used by the brothers Lumière

A scene from the film, "Rescued by Rover", 1904

ker" (so called because those early films jumped and flickered in a very distracting way. You may still hear people talk of "going to the flicks"—well, that's how the word came to be used). *The Great Train Robbery* was the first American moving picture to make any impression, and according to his son, Lasky said, "If we couldn't make a better picture than that we shouldn't be in show business."

Lasky and de Mille did make better pictures, and many of them, but they began by renting a barn in a place called Hollywood for seventy-five dollars a month. A barn, a truck and a camera were the beginnings of the great Hollywood story. It began in California for a very simple reason—people filming then had no means of artificial lighting and California had a very sunny climate. In

This is where Hollywood began

England, films were slowly gaining ground. The Lumières were wrong, the bioscope shows grew and grew. Short "flickers" were shown everywhere and anywhere. As well as winding up the bill of variety at a Music Hall, moving pictures were taken round by travelling showmen with their portable theatres (of which the largest could hold 800 people) and they put them up alongside the bearded lady and the two-headed monster in fairgrounds. Moving pictures were a new wonder of the world!

They were shown in church halls, village halls, schools, and finally in empty shops with windows knocked out and grand portico fronts put in. Weekly shows ran serials which had cliff-hanging endings: the heroine strapped to a railway line with a train approaching, or the hero lashed to a chair whilst fire raged around him. Each film-maker tried to invent some new tragedy from which the main character couldn't possibly escape, until next week!

Early and rather primitive picture houses began to spring up, usually adapted from some other kind of building, and the fire risk was great. The electrical systems were primitive, and the nitrate film was extremely inflammable; this film was often allowed to unreel into a box on the floor beneath the projector. Children were still the mainstay of the audiences, and disasters did happen, though it seems mostly because of panic rather than actual fires. In rushes to get out of buildings people were crushed, injured and killed, so safety regulations began to be introduced in 1909 and 1910.

Can you imagine going to the pictures in those early 1900s? First of all it was exciting. As exciting as seeing the first man walking on the moon, and then rushing out and looking at the moon in the sky and not really being able

26

to believe it. How could people be in a lighted square on a screen, where they could be seen walking about, while trains were shunting, and horses were galloping over broad plains, and the scenes were changing in the blink of an eye? And all for a penny!

It was truly magical, and the people flocked to see the miracle. The more people, the more kinemas, and then, as happened with the Music Hall, the attraction began to interest better-off people, and picture houses became picture palaces, and what grand palaces they were!

When the Cinema House opened in Oxford Street in London, a glittering fashionable audience arrived on the first night and found a theatre with seats of pink velvet, surrounded by oak panelling. As they had arrived and had been welcomed in an elegant foyer by liveried attendants got up like Royal Footmen, they had been filmed, and later they saw themselves miraculously reproduced on the screen.

How many times have you heard parents and maybe teachers say that television stops people reading, going to the theatre, or church, and even stops conversation? They said just the same things about the cinema in those early days, and worse. The darkness itself (necessary for projecting a film by light onto a screen) was thought dangerous and immoral. The gangster films were considered a bad example; one poor boy in 1910 went home and hanged himself after watching a particularly nasty film in London. There were

The interior of an early cinema—the best seats appear to be at the front. (You can see the projectors at the back of the cinema)

no rules about the type of films children should or should not be allowed to see, and no "A" or "X" Certificates as we know them today.

You could not only have got in for a penny, but sometimes for a clean glass bottle or jar! Presumably the kinema manager could sell them afterwards. You would have seen flickering, fast and jerkily-moving silent figures acting out exciting or funny little films like *The Schoolmaster's Portrait*, *Leap Frog*, or *A Daring Daylight Robbery*, whilst the pianist played suitable music matched to what was happening on the screen; between each scene a card would appear on which was written the words which the actors were mouthing.

In a special book of piano melodies for films called *Filmelodies*, *Photo-Play Music* by Montague Ewing, there are pieces for every possible kind of scene.

1. Scandal (chattering and quarrelling scenes)
2. Oriental Shadows (sinister Oriental scenes)
3. In the Night (stealthy night scenes)
4. Guilt (dramatic agitato)
5. Busybodies (chatter, hurry, scenes of movement)

Sometimes there was a small orchestra instead of a solo piano, and sometimes the music got a bit behind, and a tender love scene would be accompanied by galloping hooves on the piano!

There were many different sorts of films, including "naughty" ones from France and Germany, and newsreel from the Boer War, which, though not exactly entertainment, did bring in audiences hoping to see their loved ones en route for South Africa. And there were just as many different kinds of picture houses. A free cup of tea was often served, and in the very smart ones, ladies could have a shilling's worth of tea on a tray whilst watching the great comic actor, Charlie Chaplin, or Theda Bara or Mary Pickford, pin-ups of the early films. In poorer houses, oranges and crisps were eaten (imagine the noise!) and, of course, as nowadays, lots of ice-cream.

A magazine called *Kine Weekly* was very concerned to raise the tone of the "flickers" and put out a booklet in 1911, advising proprietors of kinemas to be sober and responsible, and their female attendants to wear black dresses, white caps and aprons, just like the servants in private houses.

Film soon became popular entertainment, a two-hour film of *Quo Vadis* had been made in Italy in 1912, and after the First World War the film business was to grow into a big business, with a whole world of its own of "stars", directors and new ideas.

As well as sitting in a theatre or cinema seat, people also entertained themselves, just as we do now: by dancing. Ladies and gentlemen had been 1-2-3'ing their way through waltzes for years and years, and 1-2-3-hopping round the elegant ballrooms in polka-time if they were young and energetic. Then there were group dances, done by several pairs together, like Quadrilles and Lancers, and other jerky little dances like the Military Two-Step; in fact many of these are still done at Old Tyme Dances today.

Most dancing in the early years of the century was done privately at great houses, and much etiquette was involved in going to a Grand Ball. The ladies wore beautiful ball gowns and the gentlemen sported capes and top hats. There were footmen, with powdered wigs and padded calves to make them look impressive, and ladies' maids and pages. It was all part of the way one behaved in fashionable society.

There were also less grand dances, for instance at Holborn Town Hall in London, where less well-off people (but not the really poor) danced to "The Most Select Band in London" on a chalk-powdered floor, with a Master of Ceremonies announcing the dances, and the inevitable waltz over and over again. Shaw Desmond, a writer who lived during this period, describes a conversation with his partner at just such a dance:

"... with a low, slow bow to my prospective partner, I murmur 'Ours I think!' ... once again, my noble nose poking out above my partner's shoulder ... do I hold my fair burden at the regulation ten inches from

Stars from the early days of Hollywood; from left to right: Mary Pickford, D.W. Griffiths (a film director), Charlie Chaplin and Douglas Fairbanks

contact with my manly form . . . I am whispering again 'Frightfully warm, isn't it? . . . How packed the floor seems tonight . . . Do you reverse?' . . . and (boldly) . . . 'I think we might go it regardless and regale ourselves with a whole bottle of lemonade.' "

The language might seem very strange to you now, but in those days people were much more formal with each other, more polite, some say! And isn't it funny that they should consider a *whole* bottle of lemonade a treat? Perhaps Shaw Desmond was "sending up" the grander people at smart dances who would stop whirling round the floor to drink a bottle of "bubbly" (champagne).

Then came Ragtime. *Hullo Ragtime!* was the name of a smash hit musical in 1912 and the music came from America, where it was supposedly based on a mixture of old Negro rhythms and hymn tunes. Whatever its origins, it hit this country like a hurricane!

Ragtime was the rage, to tunes with names like "Haunting Rag", "Grizzly Bear Rag", "The Bunny Hug", and the smart set did a funny sort of walking-up-and-down dancing with various bends and twists according to the latest craze. Ragtime echoed the sound of the banjo, and the early British jazz bands used the ragtime sound, as well as the Dixie-land Negro jazz bands in America.

Then just before the war, a couple called Vernon and Irene Castle—he was English and she American—began to develop the ragtime dances into something a little more graceful, and they gave demonstrations in large ballrooms and hotels to a public which was eager to learn.

The dances which emerged were the fox-trot, quickstep, a much slower waltz, and the tango. Ballroom dancing was popular by 1914, but the great age of dancing was to follow after the First World War.

The song cover for "Hullo Ragtime"

"Pack Up Your Troubles . . ."

WAR! The great and horrible First World War was about to begin. In August 1914 war was declared between England and Germany, and the nation's young men were keen to be off for they hoped to finish the unpleasant business by Christmas. People did not see this latest argument with Germany as being very important.

When war was only a matter of weeks away *The Times* said, "The domestic servant problem is one of the most serious problems of the present day." That was how the rich felt about their world, and when the war actually began men went off to enlist as soldiers as if it were some kind of patriotic lark.

Enthusiasm for the cinema, which was already growing, was immediately increased. Training camps were full of soldiers who were bored and lonely after the first thrill of joining up. The pubs had to close early to restrict the sale of alcohol to troops, so the only place to go was the "flickers".

Soldiers from the Colonies (Canada, Australia, etc.) came to this country for short periods of training or en route to the Front, and feeling lonely and strange, they found comfort in the warmth, darkness and excitement of the cinema—as did our own soldiers home on leave, for whom the cinema was a much more sympathetic place for cuddling their girlfriends than the noisy, brightly lit Music Hall.

When fathers were away at the war, children were not so strictly ruled at home, and they were allowed to go to the pictures more often. Big brothers and sisters, earning more money for jobs that had been done by the enlisted men, could spend it on frequent trips to the cinema. Early war-widows would go to "lose themselves" in a good film to forget their grief for a while, and they would often take a baby with them.

In 1916, two years after the war began (it was a forlorn hope that it would be "over by Christmas"), cinema attendances all over the country reached one billion (one thousand million). One billion! Think of that, when you go to a film and find yourself perhaps one of twenty-odd people in a huge, barn-like cinema.

When the men had gone off to the war, women did all kinds of jobs which wouldn't have been considered suitable for them before. There were women operating projection equipment (the actual machinery for showing the films), and in the Imperial Playhouse, King's Road, Chelsea in London, patrons were greeted in the foyer by a very impressive lady commissionaire wearing a uniform and waving an ebony wand.

Some small rural picture houses had to close, because of lack of staff, and no new picture palaces were built. It was thought wrong to spend money lavishly on entertainment, when as much as possible was needed for the war effort.

Although the cinema seemed to be doing quite a good job in cheering up the nation, comforting widows and putting on recruiting films, and appealing for the Red Cross and

National Relief Funds; there were still people who complained that films were bad for both children and grown-ups. A clergyman wrote to *The Times* on 5 July 1915: "They (picture palaces) are probably a more serious menace to the nation now than even drink."

Children would pass the time between school and the family evening meal by going to the pictures, and this was not thought a good thing in spite of the fact that cinemas were warmer than the streets where many poor children would otherwise have played. Others complained that the time wasted in the cinema could have been better employed in making arms in the munitions factory. But English people felt united in this time of war by laughing at the same films and sharing the same excitement of a daring adventure story. Whilst in Germany specially cheap or free showings of informational war films were put on for civilians and soldiers, in England all classes and kinds of people went to laugh together at Charlie Chaplin's latest antics.

American films were much in demand. In the early years of the war British film makers were still making films, but by the end, because of lack of money, or perhaps lack of originality, the British film industry was not doing very well.

Early in the war, Cecil Hepworth, who had made *Rescued by Rover*, used existing plays and novels and adapted them to the screen. This is nothing new to us, since television has gobbled up so many "classic" stories for its serials. But in the 1914-18 period, those lonely soldiers and their stay-at-home wives were seeing film versions of stories which they may have read, but more probably had not. There was *Far from the Madding Crowd* by Thomas Hardy (not, of course, the latest film version you see today), *Barnaby Rudge* based on the book by Charles Dickens, and in all, 500 films were made by Hepworth based on existing material, and these brought well-known plays and books to a new audience.

They had "stars", and Cecil Hepworth, who was a good publicity man, as well as a film-maker, used the new film magazines to popularise his favourites of the time. Stewart Rome and Lionelle Howard were the unlikely names of two of the actors and actresses belonging to Hepworth's studio.

There were other film-makers, of course, and accounts of their early work and the trials and tribulations they suffered show how very different the world of filming was then, compared with the huge, sophisticated industry it is today.

One colourful-sounding character was Will Barker, who had seen the impressive American film *Birth of a Nation*, (described now as the first "epic", and made by a famous director, D. W. Griffiths), and Will decided he too would make a film spectacular. He chose a story of the British Civil War in the seventeenth century, *Jane Shore*, and he intended to have an immense cast of actors and actresses for a battle scene, the Battle of Marston Moor.

He decided to take 5,000 people to Devil's Dyke in Sussex where the countryside was suitable; and then he faced an unexpected problem. Perhaps out of boredom, or made merry by the Sussex air, the cast of thousands spent far too much time in the local pubs, and were incapable when it came to fighting battles—even if only mock battles! Will Barker had another bright idea. He paid the pubs to shut during the three days' filming, and appealed to the local police to help him keep his unruly lot in order. But the local authorities refused, and Will Barker—never, it seems, at a loss for a bright idea—dressed up twelve actors in policemen's uniforms so that order was maintained.

The filming of *Jane Shore* sounds great fun and quite dramatic, doesn't it? But apparently the film our cinema-goers saw when *Jane Shore* was released, was pretty heavy-going, long and boring, and the performances from the actors were so "hammy" that audiences burst out laughing. *Jane Shore* was not a great success.

This point about over-acting is interesting for us, because in those days of early films, the film-makers would bring in famous names from the stage like Gerald du Maurier, Ellaline Terriss, or Gladys Cooper, and hope

A lull in the fighting—a scene from the film "Jane Shore"

they would draw audiences in the same way that big stars can make a film successful today.

What had to be learned, and it was a difficult lesson for highly successful theatre actors and actresses, was that a completely different style of acting was required for the moving pictures. The camera picked up every movement and acting had to be much more underplayed and less dramatic. You can often see how exaggerated the old style of acting looks when early films are shown on television. Cecil Hepworth says in his autobiography that he had great difficulty persuading his stars not to put on stage make-up, which was very thick and heavy so that it could be seen from the back of a theatre, but in close-up on the cinema screen it could look like a hideous mask.

Two stars who became popular were Alma Taylor and Chrissie White. They started as a couple of tomboy teenage girls, and one film shows them delightedly soaking a group of pursuers with a jet of water from a fire-hose. When they grew too old for such childish tricks, they were given other starring roles and were great favourites with the British public.

In various ways the war was a subject for newsreels and propaganda films, which sug-

33

War propaganda movie, subsidized by British Government, for U.S. consumption, starred the Gish sisters as victims of brutal Prussians. It was directed by another American, D. W. Griffith.

A scene from a War propaganda film

gested that the war seemed to be going better for us than perhaps it was. There were some dreadful little "shorts" made in a few days, about Daddy going to the war, about a German spy being captured, and other rather unlikely but patriotic tales of daring rescues and heroic deeds.

Newsreels themselves, filmed at the places where the war was actually being fought, were a different matter. British cameramen had grown fed-up with not being allowed to go where they wanted, and in 1915 a War Office agreement got these men to the Front, and a twice-weekly newsreel was assembled called *Whirlpool of War*.

Long feature films about the war were made, and the most famous was *The Battle of the Somme*, shot in July 1916. Can you imagine the effect on those left at home, with no nightly television or radio news broadcasts, and with newspaper reports that often selected only the good news? Here was film of their sons and husbands actually fighting in the mud, tanks crawling along across battlefields and troops being killed. Not everyone approved. One cinema manager refused to show the film, saying he had a "place of entertainment, not a chamber of horrors". But over 2,000 other cinemas took *The Battle of the Somme*, and the cinema queues to see it were the longest ever known. There was no sound, of course, but frequent subtitles came up on the screen to tell the audience what was happening.

In spite of British successes in war filming, American moving pictures were rapidly gaining popularity and taking over the market for screen adventure and romance. By 1918, British film-making had come to a standstill, and the way was clear for the Hollywood take-over.

Although British film-makers were in the doldrums, the British public were still great film-goers, and the movies, far from remaining what the Lumière Brothers thought would be a nine-day wonder, had become an established and necessary part of the British way of life.

What was happening in the Music Hall during these war years? As you can imagine, the energy and rumbustious nature of the Music Hall audience and artists was immediately directed towards helping along the war effort.

Patriotic songs were written, like "Jolly Good Luck to the Girl who Loves a Soldier", and

> I do like you cocky when you've got your Khaki on,
> I do feel so proud of you, I do, honour bright,
> I'm going to give you an extra cuddle tonight.

There were jokes and sketches which whipped up anti-German feeling, and though at first they were popular, very soon audiences —particularly soldiers back from the Front— began to dislike the crude war jokes which seemed to be out of touch with the awful killing and suffering that was going on at the scenes of battle. A famous poet of the time, Siegfried Sassoon, wrote a poem after a visit to the Music Hall wishing a tank would go

Harry Lauder in his stage outfit

clattering down the theatre aisle and "blow the place to smithereens".

Songs in the Music Hall grew sad and some attempted to cheer up the worried, like "Pack up your Troubles in your old Kit Bag and Smile, Smile, Smile", or "Goodbye Dolly, I must leave you", and "Keep right on to the end of the road". This last song was made famous by Harry Lauder, a Music Hall star from Scotland who became very rich, with a castle called Lauder Ha', and who led a high life hobnobbing with the President and millionaires in America. He was useful in the war effort, since he could do his best to persuade the Americans to join in the war on our side. He eventually became Sir Harry Lauder and made many gramophone records and early radio broadcasts. It is a curious fact that music hall artists in general were very scared of the gramophone as a threat to their livelihood. They thought if people could hear the songs at home, they'd stop going to the Music Hall. Harry Lauder, however, was canny enough to see the advantages, and when he toured abroad, everyone knew him from his gramophone records, royalties from which had already made money for him. Two new popular entertainments had suddenly appeared: gramophone records and radio—more of these later.

The theatre survived very well during the war years of 1914-18. Patriotism was present on the stage too, and an odd entertainment called *England Expects*, half dramatic sketches and half musical, was put on at the Stoll Theatre in London. There was also the same feeling of escaping from a gloomy atmosphere, as in the cinema. People tried to forget their troubles for a while when they set off for the theatre. Business was carried on as usual, as far as possible, and special wartime theatre events were organised.

After the Americans came into the war on our side, there was free entertainment for American and British troops at the Palace Theatre in London, every Sunday evening. This was not only to cheer them up, but also to get them together in a friendly way. These shows were the very best that British theatre had to offer, since all the London theatre managers agreed to take turns at staging them. There was great variety in the kind of shows the soldiers saw—one week an evening of opera, the next a colourful musical revue, and then perhaps the next Sunday would see Thomas Beecham's orchestra filling the stage and overflowing into the front rows of seats.

The Americans were to be made welcome, and they got all the best seats: the stalls, the grand circle and the boxes. Up in the gallery and the upper circle were the British troops, who before the show would release hundreds of balloons, so that the Americans below could burst them with cigarettes or their hands, to the sound of much cheering and whooping.

Although the shows were a huge success, the original object of fostering friendship between British and American troops did not make much headway.

The famous actor/manager Seymour Hicks and his wife Ellaline Terriss went to entertain the troops in France, as did Harry Lauder and others from the Music Hall. Some entertainers helped to recruit soldiers; on the page opposite you can see the well-known actress, Violet Loraine, helping to recruit.

In the theatre as well as in other walks of life, women were taking over men's jobs and two quite famous actresses, Gladys Cooper and Marie Lohr, both became managers of theatres as well as acting in the plays.

By the beginning of the First World War, a kind of entertainment called revue had become very popular, and was taking the place of the old Music Hall variety and to some extent ousting the musical comedies like *The Merry Widow*, although in 1916, a musical called *Chu-Chin-Chow* opened which was a record-breaking success.

Revue was a name given to all sorts of different hotchpotch entertainments, but the best ones were full of witty jokes, nice music, beautiful girls and costumes. The most famous of the revue producers was Sir Charles Cochran, who put on *Odds and Ends* in 1914. It was supposed to rely for its success more on cleverness and wit than on spectacular costumes and scenery. He followed it up with

Violet Loraine, the actress, recruiting in Trafalgar Square in August, 1915

many more, and his Cochran Young Ladies were as sought after as the Gaiety Girls had been a few years before.

In one respect the theatre was unchanged by war—the personalities of the stage could ignore the quarrels between countries. George Edwardes had built up the Gaiety's remarkable success with *The Merry Widow*, which had been written by a German called Franz Lehar, who was still living in Germany during the war. When George Edwardes died in 1915, Franz Lehar and other German composers who had worked with "The Guv'nor" (as Edwardes was known), sent a huge wreath to England, and as the war was well and truly on, and German security very tight, nobody ever found out how it had been smuggled across Europe.

Revue and musical comedy were especially popular in wartime, since they were cheerful and colourful with tuneful songs and brilliant scenes which took people's minds off their worrying everyday lives.

Some First World War revue songs are still sung, and vary from "Somebody Knows—Somebody Cares" and "When Irish Eyes are Smiling" to "Naughty, Naughty One, Gerrard" and "Oh, You Beautiful Doll". Two of the most famous were "Roses of Picardy" (Picardy is in France, where the battles were being fought) and "Mademoiselle from Armentieres", which had little phrases of terrible English/French like "Inky-Pinky-Parlez-Vous" showing how the English soldiers were having trouble with an unfamiliar language. In matters of love, they were overcoming their troubles pretty well!

Melodrama was also influenced by the war, and the plots became more up-to-date. At the Lyceum, a play called *Seven Days' Leave* ran for

711 performances. In those days of fighting and loneliness, when soldiers missed their families, and wives were worrying about their husbands, the idea of seven days' leave must have been heaven.

There were changes in the audiences, too. London was blacked out totally when a show called *Tonight's the Night* opened on 14 April 1915 (with a "low" comedian called Leslie Henson whose speciality was a hoarse froggy voice). There were no sparkling lights or glitter outside the theatre. German air-raids were taken very seriously. And inside, where were our elegant ladies and gentlemen? Not a single evening dress to be seen, and as most of the theatre-goers were workers in munitions factories and soldiers home on leave, the general appearance of the audience was dreary and drab.

They had come to the theatre to be lifted out of themselves, and the show was gay, fast and amusing. One turn, "They'll Never Believe Me" had a lovely haunting melody which must have touched many hearts in the audience on that first night in 1915, and on many occasions since:

And when I tell them—
And I'm certainly going to tell them—
That I'm the man whose wife one day you'll be,
They'll never believe me—
They'll never believe me—
That from this great big world you've chosen me.

For a young soldier off to the war with a good chance of being killed, this must have been a very moving lyric.

The Cinema Years

Inside a Picture Palace—the Astoria at Finsbury Park. Imagine trying to concentrate on the film in such lavish surroundings as these!

On 11 November 1918, the First World War came to an end with a great popular entertainment which was totally free: from every street corner there came the sound of "maroons"—very loud, cracking fireworks. These had been used to warn people that German bombers were on their way, but now they signalled the end of the war, and everyone went mad with joy.

Into the streets rushed office workers and shopkeepers, and everyone else who could safely leave their post. There was yelling and cheering, and street-sellers did a roaring trade in special sausage-shaped balloons called "Zepps", named after the German airship Zeppelins. The balloons were then thrown into the air and exploded to add to the general noise and confusion.

All this rejoicing was understandable. There would be no more fighting in the mud of Flanders and no more senseless killing of young men, both German and English.

Everyone felt a great relief that it was all over.

But in Britain, things were not going to go back to normal immediately. This chapter is called The Cinema Years, but it really means the Hollywood cinema years. As far as British film-making was concerned, things had more or less come to a halt by the end of the war.

What the British did do after the First World War, was to begin to build Picture Palaces again. There was even more longing for escape into a glamorous world, as post-war countries are drab and austere. Money and men have been used up, and after the

A mighty cinema organ

Rudolph Valentino in "The Son of the Sheik". (He was one of the first cinema heart-throbs)

excitement of victory is over, all that is left is the hard work of restoring the country to normal again.

Mr Sol Levy, a rich man with an eye for future profit, built up his Futurist Cinema in Birmingham, and followed it with the Broadway Paladium at Ealing, the Kilburn Grange Picture House, and others which were all equally luxurious. Outside they were resplendent with Grecian columns, shiny black glass, or Moorish arches, and the insides were decorated with a gorgeous mixture of Chinese lanterns and dragons, Japanese butterflies, mermaids and goldfish, English medieval shields, pennants and coats of armour, or an entirely Egyptian decor. If you turn back to page 39, you can see the interior of the Astoria at Finsbury Park.

Before the performance, an overture would be played on a mighty cinema organ (see page 40) which rose up from the depths in front of the screen and which had changing coloured lights. As well as music, there were endless special effects: bells, tom-toms, wind, thunder —nothing was too ambitious for the cinema organ.

And what films did the eager audiences see? The years of the star had arrived. It seems strange to us, but in the beginning of film-making none of the actors was named, then gradually one or two became familiar to cinema audiences for their comic performances, or for being especially attractive.

In the 1920s, the film star with the greatest fan club of all time had appeared: Rudolph Valentino. He was worshipped by women of all ages. Even now there is a Rudolph Valentino Fan Club. Look at the picture of him on the previous page. Can you see why he seemed so glamorous? There are film clips of his acting, and his style seems very exaggerated and even comical to our modern eyes. But that was the fashion, and every young man wanted to look like Rudolph Valentino and every girl dreamed of being carried off through the desert on a beautiful Arab horse, clasped in the arms of Sheik Rudolph Valentino.

When he died at the age of thirty-one, in 1926, after only six years in films, his body was carried back from New York to Hollywood and all along the railway track stood crowds of weeping women. He represented Hollywood stardom at its peak.

Other favourites with British audiences were comedians like Charlie Chaplin, Harold Lloyd, Buster Keaton, and the Marx Brothers. Films were made quickly and cheaply, and comedy films were enormously popular in the days when there was still no talking, only the old piano-player or orchestra pounding away beneath the screen.

There were girl heart-throbs too, of course. Clara Bow, called the "It Girl", was one of the first and all the girls in the audience tried to imitate her round eyes and the cupid's bow mouth. Greta Garbo was truly beautiful, but shy and overwhelmed by Hollywood, and her catch-phrase became "I want to be alone". Mary Pickford was known as "America's Sweetheart" and became leader of the Hollywood top set socially, along with her husband, Douglas Fairbanks. They would give wild and glamorous parties at their house called Pickfair. It was everyone's aim to get Rudolph Valentino to a party, he loved dancing, and did a sensational tango, and wouldn't go to houses where there wasn't a dance floor. This is why some of the fantastic Hollywood houses still have small, elegantly black-and-white tiled dance floors.

Serials like *The Perils of Pauline* were still popular. Every week there would be a different episode, and at the end of each instalment Pearl White was left in a hopelessly dangerous situation! She might be tied down to railway lines with the train fast approaching, or about to be attacked by a fierce beast or a raving madman. Audiences couldn't wait to see next week's instalment, and girls who saw the films used to go home and act out the entire episode all over again, with themselves in the heroine's part, of course.

In silent movies, stunts were especially popular. Stuntmen were in great demand and the work was really dangerous. Joe Rock, a well-known stuntman, had a marvellous story of being hired to take part in a mock crowd-

Another heart-throb—Clara Bow, the "It Girl"

The Marx Brothers

fight scene. Rows of bruisers were lined up and told to begin "fighting" when the director blew the whistle, and to stop when he blew the whistle a second time. The whistle was duly blown, and the tough guys began to fight. The fighting grew fast and furious, and when the "stop" whistle blew no-one took any notice. Studio lights were switched on and off to try and stop them, a whole orchestra ready for the next scene was swept off the platform, the fight became a riot and spread out into the courtyard, and finally police were called to close the scene.

That was early film-making, and it is difficult to imagine it happening now. Those days were rougher and tougher and the audiences loved tales of a Hollywood that seemed much larger than life.

Hollywood rapidly became a legendary place. From that barn of Jesse Lasky's we talked about earlier, Hollywood grew into a fabulous mecca where all actors and actresses went to be stars. Many never made it, but those that reached stardom were admired and copied all over the world. The cinema really began to influence the way people looked and dressed. In old photographs you can see how ordinary girls in the street copied their favourite stars' make-up, hair styles and even the expressions on their faces. Winifred Foley, who wrote a book about her childhood in the Forest of Dean, remembers her sister saying to her "Let me do thee up like Mary Pickford." Somehow, said Winifred Foley, her sister managed to tie round her head every bit of a parcel of ribbon pieces sent by an aunt. "My gawd," said the sister, "I reckon thee'st do look better'n Mary Pickford—more like a fairy queen."

So you see how even children living in remote country areas in England were well aware of the latest "Mary Pickford Look"; and in the 1920s, the great craze for getting a really rich suntan was partially a result of the dashing Douglas Fairbanks having a romantically dark complexion.

Not all the stars were sophisticated grown-ups, however. Nowadays there aren't many child stars and rules on education in stage schools are strict. In Hollywood's silent days, and when the talkies came later, child stars were in great demand. There was a series of comedies made by an American, Hal Roach, using a group of children called *Our Gang*. The actors in *Our Gang* had a special school paid for by the film studio.

Children were required to act and dance and, most difficult, to cry. A story about Jackie Cooper, a famous child star of the day, tells how he just could not squeeze out the tears for a particular scene in a film called *Peck's Bad Boy*, and even when he was told his dog had been run over he suspected a trick. Finally the director (who was Jackie's greatest friend) was blamed and threatened with the sack. So Jackie wept at last . . . yes, it does sound like singing violins and a lot of sentimental nonsense; but that's how Hollywood was, and how the audiences were. They loved the soppy romances and happy endings which you probably laugh at when you see old films on television today.

The movies had become part of everyday life, when, after one or two false starts, along came the "Talkies".

The very first sound picture was *The Jazz Singer* made in 1927, starring Al Jolson singing sentimental songs and talking to his beloved Mammy. Many talking pictures soon followed, and the excitement of the new craze was just as hectic as when the first silent movies caught on.

One elderly man remembers being in St. Albans when the first talking picture arrived at one of the town's cinemas. The rival cinema, on the opposite side of the road and still showing silent movies, put up a large banner across the front of the cinema, which said in gold letters "SILENCE IS GOLDEN"; but the talkies were here to stay, and immediately a great many film stars fell out of favour, because although they were beautiful or handsome, with great acting ability and wonderfully expressive faces, they had terrible voices!

You may have seen *Singing in the Rain* with Gene Kelly which is often shown on television, and although this film was made in 1952, it is

"Our Gang"

about film-making in the 1920s and has a gorgeous blonde who was just such an actress, an absolute bombshell to look at, but when she opened her mouth, out came a tiny nasal squeak which ruined everything!

By the 1930s, silent movies were finished, although the great Charlie Chaplin did not speak in a film until 1940. Somehow silence was an important part of his comic/sad clown kind of humour, and the expressions on his face said everything that was needed.

Hollywood in the thirties was an enormous mushroom of success, growing and growing, and vast amounts of money were made by movie "moguls" or "tycoons" like Cecil B. de Mille, Samuel Goldwyn and Jesse J. Lasky. They had very grand ways of carrying on, hiring and firing their employees at the flick of a cigar ash, and reputedly helping to elect American Presidents.

Whether this was so or not, the film tycoons had a great deal of power in the movie world, and rumours like Cecil B. de Mille having solid gold bath taps were circulated by magazines and newspapers, who also delighted in the bizarre way he dressed, as a cross between a circus ring-master and a cavalry officer. Cecil B. de Mille would arrive at his office in well-cut flared riding-breeches, round his waist a belt from which hung watches that told him what time it was in all parts of the world. In his pocket he jangled (more furiously as his temper rose) a collection of old golden twenty-dollar pieces. He had monumental rages, and periods of such charm and sweetness that no woman could

Cecil B. de Mille (on the left) with visitors to the set of "The King of Kings", 1927

resist him!

These were days in Hollywood when life was very enjoyable and glamorous for a film star or a director at the top of the Hollywood tree. Film fans went to the cinema twice, or often three times a week, to have some of that glamour and excitement rub off on to them.

"It was heaven to us", said an old man, remembering his visits to a cinema in Peterborough. "The outside was shiny black, and you pushed through the swing doors into a foyer brightly lit with a twinkling fountain in the middle. The usherettes were all nice clean-looking girls, polite and helpful, and smart in their uniforms."

A group of lads and girls would first go to have tea in the cinema restaurant, which was upstairs and had windows overlooking the street. An orchestra would very likely be playing on a little platform in one corner of the restaurant, usually tunes from the latest musical film, and after a pot of tea for four, bread and butter and jam and perhaps some biscuits, the group would move into the cinema itself to see an early Deanna Durbin or Judy Garland film. Most children of the time, and grown-ups, were delighted by Judy Garland in *The Wizard of Oz*, a musical based

Judy Garland (as Dorothy), the Tin Man and the Scarecrow in a scene from "The Wizard of Oz"

on a fairy story for children which is still worth seeing today. These were both pretty teenage singers who became great stars. Deanna Durbin faded before Judy Garland, and since Judy's sad death at the end of a not-too-happy life, her daughter, Liza Minelli, has carried on her mother's brilliant singing, dancing and acting talents.

Or they might have seen the latest Shirley Temple film. Shirley Temple was a curly haired cutie who danced and lisped and simpered her way through a dozen or so sentimental comedies from the age of five!

These young people out for a Saturday afternoon and evening's entertainment in Peterborough in the 1930s could have seen the great dancing couple, Fred Astaire and Ginger Rogers, in one of their musical comedy films, *Top Hat*, *The Gay Divorce*, or *Shall We Dance?*

Dancing was still a major pleasure in most young people's lives, and all the lads with shiny shoes, sleek black hair and baggy trousers, tried to dance like Fred Astaire. His tap-dancing was perfectly rhythmic and technically brilliant, and his movements were so graceful and supple that he seemed at times to have no bones at all in his agile body. Try to see an old film with Astaire on television; there is no-one to touch him for classy, elegant Hollywood dancing.

And in their imaginations every boy's partner was a Ginger Rogers. She floated weightlessly on tip-toes, spun round in a cloud of white tulle, was lifted high into the air by Fred, and landed with not the teeniest bump. All effortlessly beautiful and graceful, and a delightful daydream for a group of youngsters sitting in the one and threepenny's holding hands and sighing with delight. Hollywood manufactured dreamland, whether it was Westerns, Bible epics, or the slapstick humour of Harold Lloyd, Buster Keaton and Charlie Chaplin, and that is what the cinema-goers expected to see. They followed the fortunes of their favourite star's personal lives in fan magazines, and judging from dozens of cartoons from Punch magazine at the time, most of Hollywood life was spent in getting

A poster advertising the film, "Top Hat"

married, divorced, re-married, and divorced again, and so on!

The American influence was so strong that responsible people worried that the English language might be lowered to an American nasal twang, and in 1932 someone wrote to *The Times* suggesting that a national campaign to "Speak British" be adopted. There were protests about film language, morals, violence, and politics, but the audience also continued to enjoy the cinema enormously.

Colour came to the screen. Technicolour was first used fully in 1933, by Walt Disney in one of a series of cartoons he made called *Silly Symphonies*. This one was *Flowers and Trees* and must have been as exciting as the first time we saw colour on our television screens.

Walt Disney was a household name in the thirties and still is. Donald Duck, Mickey Mouse, Snow White and the Seven Dwarfs, and Pinnochio were all wonderfully animated films made with an imagination which created positive and special characters from the heroes, giving Disney many well-deserved Academy Awards.

Snow White and the Seven Dwarfs (classified A) was seen in forty-one different countries, in ten different languages, and is an example of what this book is all about: popular entertainment for very large numbers of people. Everyone went around singing the songs from

the film: "Whistle While you Work", "Hi-ho, Hi-ho, It's Off to Work We Go" and "Some Day my Prince will Come"; and everyone had the same experience of terror when the wicked black-hooded witch with her long-clawed hands cast her evil spells. *Snow White* was popular with all ages, but there were also special children's film shows, which come later in our story.

In the 1930s the British film industry was not completely eclipsed by Hollywood, and was eventually rescued from its "second-best" position by a sensible film-maker called Alexander Korda who decided that the only way to beat 'em was to join 'em. He made a highly successful spectacular film called *The Private Life of Henry VIII*, and those of you who remember that Henry had six wives, can

The wicked witch giving Snow White a poisoned apple

The banqueting scene from "The Private Life of Henry VIII". (King Henry is talking to Catherine Howard)

imagine what the Private Life was about. Owing to a flamboyant, Hollywood style of production, this film was a triumph in America as well as in Britain.

There were also popular British stars like Gracie Fields, a singer from Lancashire, who appeared in cheerful comedy films singing earthy songs.

Another British star was Will Hay who came to films from Music Hall; his speciality was playing a seedy, useless schoolmaster. Many of his films are now regarded as classic comedies of those times. And also from the Halls came George Formby Junior, the talented son of Little Willie from Lancashire. He was phenomenally successful, with his toothy grin, his knack of encountering misfortune, and his ukelele. His songs with a

jangling, relentless accompaniment, could be heard coming from countless open windows on a summer's afternoon, from gramophone records playing "When I'm Cleaning Windows", "Leaning on a Lamp-post at the Corner of the Street", "Chinese Laundry Blues" and many, many more. George had a very managing wife, who kept him in order and made sure of his success—or maybe "bossed him around" would be a better description!

Thrillers were very popular, and one of the most famous was called *The Ghost Train*; it was originally a stage play which was made into a silent movie in 1929, then produced again as a talkie in 1931. The original play was written by the actor Arnold Ridley who may be known to you as Private Godfrey in

Another Picture Palace—the Astoria, Brixton. All the signs would be lit up at night; there were even strips of lighting on the dome.

television's *Dad's Army* series, and it was revived at Christmas 1976, at the Old Vic Theatre in London, where it was as exciting and frightening as ever. *The Ghost Train* is a good example of how various forms of popular entertainment can use the same good material with equal success.

Film-going continued to be the most popular means of entertainment for most people in the miserable 1930s. Just as going to the pictures had been a way of cheering up people who were saddened and frightened by war, so, in the Depression, cinema audiences scraped the bottom of their purses to find enough to pay for a couple of hours' escape to dreamland. When you remember that during those years people were nearly starving, and men went on demonstration marches for miles and miles until they dropped, you can perhaps realise how important the cinema was as a relief from the grim lives that people were leading.

Publicity stunts were meant to draw people's attention to a particular film. They were fun, and they were free! In the middle of Kingston High Street, a camel sat down for a rest on the way to publicise a circus film. When it got up, it decided to explore a bit, and wrecked a greengrocer's shop, frightened the life out of a milkman's horse and generally caused a great deal of laughter.

The cinema, and the cinema manager's family, were often the social centre of the town. Personal problems were sorted out there, and presents were brought to the cash desk: perhaps a bar of chocolate, a bunch of garden flowers or some tomatoes. They were all brought in appreciation of what the little Essoldo, Tivoli or Plaza meant to the customers.

Whether it was a Picture Palace like the Finsbury Park Astoria, or a more humble "bug-hutch", or even "flea-pit", it was a marvellous magical source of never-ending popular entertainment, and its spell was to last for some years yet.

The Years of the Bright Young Things

From left to right: Gertrude Laurence, Noel Coward, Adrienne Allen and Lawrence Olivier in a scene from "Private Lives" at the Phoenix Theatre, London, 1930

We look back at the twenties as a frenzied period. The war was over, and the young people who were left grew more and more pleasure-seeking. Those who knew about politics and the state of the country's finances could see hard times coming, but the Bright Young Things, as they were called, whirled and danced, gave fancy dress parties, and

The Co-optimists

didn't care a fig for anyone. In fact some think that a sort of craziness entered people, especially rich young people, who seemed to enjoy themselves at all costs.

Dancing had become more varied and lively, and in the theatre there were dozens of musical revues, from which the dance tunes came. Noel Coward was the most witty and urbane writer and performer of them all, and excelled in the revue theatre. "Tall and divinely handsome in grey" was his own description of himself and he was the master of shows like *London Calling*, which starred himself and a lovely singer called Gertrude Lawrence, who had come from very poor beginnings. When Gertrude Lawrence died in 1952, all the lights of theatreland in London and New York were lowered for three minutes as a tribute to her, so you can imagine how greatly loved and truly popular she had been.

Noel Coward invented a character in *London Calling* called Hernia Whittlebot, a "burlesque" on a famous literary threesome of the time, Sacheverell, Osbert and Edith Sitwell. Hernia Whittlebot, says Noel Coward in his autobiography, made the Sitwells very cross, and he claims innocently he never knew why! The luxurious, upper-class life of Noel Coward and his circle of friends appealed greatly to the Bright Young Things. The world of the exclusive "In" set was very small and privileged.

Another revue company was the Co-optimists. They were a kind of concert party who banded together after the war, full of optimism and ideas of sharing profits, and for a few years they were just right for theatre audiences who wanted a gay, lighthearted night out. When one of the girls in the troupe fell in love with one of the boys, their wedding

Ivor Novello—composer, writer and matinee idol

*Pavlova as the Dying Swan from the ballet,
"Swan Lake"*

was a national event. People were very interested in what they were trying to do in the revue world.

More music was flowing from a "matinee idol" composer/writer/performer called Ivor Novello. His most famous song was "Keep the Home Fires Burning", a patriotic war ballad, but he wrote and starred in shows like *Glamorous Night, Careless Rapture* and *The Dancing Years*. Those titles tell you something about the times. Longing for luxury, freedom from worry and sheer pleasure, theatre-goers worshipped Ivor Novello. The fact that he was really immensely handsome too, gave him the "matinee idol" label, a name meaning a handsome actor who could be relied upon to fill the afternoon performances with rows of adoring women! There were other matinee idols like the incredibly debonair Jack Buchanan; perhaps a similar admiration now is given to pop stars and the television heroes of American thriller series.

There was other lighthearted theatre; Ben Travers was writing farces, which were foolish, funny plays like *A Cuckoo in the Nest* (1928), with ridiculous plots, and usually a "silly ass" character who kept the audience in stitches. This sort of stupid, often aristocratic "chinless wonder" survives in the novels of P. G. Wodehouse.

There was also serious theatre for those who were not carried along by the wave of the Bright Young Things or the flappers. In the twenties and thirties, plays by Ibsen and Shakespeare, Chekhov and O'Neill were produced, as well as by extremely successful "middle-brow" writers like J. B. Priestley.

Noel Coward, the master of lighthearted revue, had also written a very serious and shocking play called *The Vortex*, about a mother having love affairs and her son taking drugs. It may not sound so shocking now, but these were unmentionable subjects in 1924, when *The Vortex* was first performed.

Patriotism could still be found in the theatre, there was still a British Empire, and it was important to keep up the national feeling of England's pride and glory. *Cavalcade*, also written by Noel Coward in the Depression time of the thirties, was a large-scale patriotic musical show, and aimed at giving back to a miserable people just this sense of pride.

Ballet was becoming more popular, and some stars such as the legendary Pavlova, whom you can see on the previous page, were in demand for touring round the Variety Theatres. This was not thought strange, for

the only ballet in London at the beginning of the century had been little dances slipped into the programmes of the Music Halls. Ballet was taken more seriously by a woman theatre manager called Lilian Baylis. She believed that Shakespeare's plays and other serious types of entertainment could appeal to everybody. She took over the Victoria Theatre in South London and created the Old Vic, a splendid exciting but serious theatre with low-priced seats. It was a great success, so she then went into a very old Islington theatre, which had once been the fairground pleasure garden called Sadler's Wells, and here she created a ballet and opera company. You can guess how

Scene from "Journey's End" at the Savoy Theatre, London, 1929

important she was when you realise that the Old Vic became the National Theatre Company, the little ballet troupe became The Royal Ballet, and the opera company became The English Opera Company.

Provincial and repertory theatres all over the country brought plays and shows to everyone who was interested in keeping up with the latest happenings in the theatre. Not all theatre was cheerful and optimistic, however. A very famous play called *Journey's End*, by R. C. Sherriff, attempted to show the war as it really had been, not romantic or heroic, but cruel and brutal, reducing the soldiers to cowards.

In spite of the misery of unemployment and war memories there was still national pride and a determination to enjoy life during the 1930s. Patriotic serious music was popular too, such as Elgar's "Spirit of England", and the "Pomp and Circumstance March", and more people were going to concerts. The Promenade Concerts, with cheap tickets and favourite classical pieces, had been started by Sir Henry Wood as early as 1895, and all sorts of music lovers gathered at the Queen's Hall to hear performers like Dame Clara Butt.

This famous singer was described as a

Gramophones became more compact, but they were still cranked by hand

"Mother of Vikings" and she looked like the prow of a ship in full sail. Her voice was distinctive, and on the existing records of her singing, she sounds like a church organ. Music was written especially for her, and she was greatly loved, not only for her musical gifts, but also for her generous nature: for she often sang to raise money for charities.

Perhaps the most popular music of all was for dancing, since more people than ever before could enjoy it through the gramophone. Ragtime, Jazz and all the variations and developments were played in the front room of nearly every suburban house, where the more compact box-shaped record player had replaced the horned Victrola. It was still cranked by hand.

The twenties and thirties *were* the dancing years. You might say that we all dance now, and people have always danced. Although this is true, dancing was an unparalleled craze during the 1920s and 30s. In villages, towns and cities, girls, boys, men and women all danced energetically or romantically to the popular tunes of the time. They danced to gramophone records and tiny amateur bands, to the wireless which by now was churning out hours of dance music, or to the famous bands themselves in hotel ballrooms or the grander Palais de Danse.

There were even dance "marathons" in which a prize was given to the couples who could dance the longest. In America these would continue for days, until the dancers passed out and fell to the floor.

The writer's father has a curious story of preparing for the village dance in Baston, in Lincolnshire. He and his pals had to take a horse-drawn wagon to a nearby village to fetch the dance floor. The dance was to be held in the school, and the floorboards there were too rough and uneven for dancing. So the lads went off to Glinton, a nearby village, and came back with numbered boards which fitted together exactly, and were put down in the schoolroom to make a smooth dance floor. He says: "We danced the Charleston, the Foxtrot and the One-Step, to a six-piece band from Stamford, and we danced till one a.m."

After the dance those boards all had to be loaded up again in numerical order and were taken back to Glinton for the next village "hop".

In a lovely book by Dolly Scannell, about her childhood in the East End of London*, she tells how she and her sister went to Town Hall dances, not only to dance, but also to meet "Mr Right", the marvellous suitor of every girl's dreams at that time; he was supposed to look and behave like a film star, but most girls settled for someone less glamorous to marry!

"The dancing was superb," she says; "these white, poker-faced young men with their creased suits which smelt of moth-balls and tom-cats, would nod their heads. 'Coming rahnd?' and off we'd go . . ."

Then in complete contrast to this were the tea-dances, where you could have afternoon tea and dance to a small orchestra; there were also dancing clubs, and the night clubs for the rich. The most famous and fashionable of these was the Kit-Kat Club, where top bands like Vincent Lopez played for £1,100 a week —a very great deal of money in those days. It was the "done thing" to be seen at the Kit-Kat. The fashionable set of debutantes and their debonair escorts with shiny smoothed-down hair and evening suits, would sway to the foxtrot, and bend and lean to the tango, in an atmosphere so smoky and crowded that it sounds almost unpleasant!

In these crowded dance clubs, new, energetic dances began to appear. Skirts became shorter and ropes of beads grew longer and in came the Charleston and the Black Bottom.

Around this time, there was a new dance, or

Dancing "The Crossword Puzzle" dance at the East Ham Palais de Danse in January, 1925

58

* Mother Knew Best by Dolly Scannell (Pan, 1974)

a new variation, every month, and dancing schools taught steps with names like "the pull-back", "the triple", and "the slaps".

Perhaps the best-remembered dancing places of all were the Palais de Danse. Palais means Palace, and the very fact that the name was French gave these dance halls an air of excitement and the possibility of romance.

Hammersmith Palais in London was the biggest and brightest and most famous of them all. Inside there was the dance floor—like an enormous skating rink—with tables round the edge, and above, a balcony where onlookers could sit and drink coffee or soft drinks, and in some of the Palais de Danse you could eat as well. On an elegantly decorated dais at one end was the band. The band leader was the hero of the evening, as was the singer who was often a regular performer with that particular band. All the famous bands of the era played at the Hammersmith Palais, under spotlights and a great revolving ball of glass prisms in the ceiling which reflected the lights. All week young people looked forward to Saturday night at the Palais! Not every dance hall was as big or smart as the Hammersmith and other Palais de Danse. Sometimes it was just a large hall with a few tables and chairs and a band at one end. But with the music and the dusty floor, cigarette smoke and the smell of Californian Poppy or Carnation scent, girls and lads enjoyed themselves just as much.

The Savoy Hotel in London was another fashionable place for dancing, and it became a favourite owing to early broadcasts of dance band music. The Savoy Orpheans were heard at the beginning of broadcasting and you will hear of them in the next chapter.

Gramophone records played a great part in the dancing years, as you can imagine, and although they may seem pretty primitive to you now, they were amazing technical achievements in their day. Perhaps we should go back a couple of steps to see how the gramophone began, and how it came to be such an important part of people's lives. The original invention in 1877 was the phonograph by Edison, whose scratchy voice saying "Mary had a little lamb" began the whole

idea of reproducing music, sound and the human voice, and once it caught on it developed rapidly. At first, records were cylindrical and the amplifier was a large horn, but soon discs were made.

Records were not too expensive, and by the thirties they were being sold for sixpence (about 2½p in today's money) from Woolworths and many other big stores, and also from music shops, where sheet music for the same songs was also on sale.

Dance music was recorded by all the top bands, and in the early days with singers who were merely "A Vocal Refrain". Then singing with a band became a desirable thing to do and names like Al Bowlly and later Bing Crosby emerged on record labels.

The early dance bands became big "swing" orchestras, playing as much to listeners as to dancers. Well known band leaders were Jack Hylton, Billy Cotton, Ambrose, Nat Gonella, and Ray Noble. The picture of Ambrose and his band (on the next page) was taken in 1932 and gives you an idea of the style and elegance of dancing in those days.

Fashions in music go around and around, and lately there has been an interest in reviving the Big Band sound of the thirties; original records can still be found if you hunt in junk shops where no collector has been before you.

The records themselves had very attractive labels in the centre, and even these are now collected and highly prized. It's strange, when you remember that a favourite game in the forties was "spinning". Children bought huge piles of those thick, shellac records for one penny, took them into cornfields behind their houses, and spun them as high and as far as possible over the stubble. They crashed into pieces at the end of their flight, collectors' items, every one!

In the days when everyone bought the latest dance tune to play on their portable or cabinet gramophone, there was another advantage for young people in this miraculous invention. In 1923, a writer commented that being able to practice the latest steps of a new dance to a gramophone record at home meant

Dancing to Ambrose and his Band at the Mayfair Hotel, London, in 1932. Look at the plush surroundings

that no-one need any longer be a "wall-flower". Do you know what a wallflower is? Not the sweet-smelling plant, but in those days when dancing was always done in twos, one boy and one girl, the worst thing that could happen to a girl, usually to one who was known to be a rotten dancer, was to be left as a wallflower, sitting by the wall and no-one asking her to dance. And a girl never asked a boy! This pairing off was managed neatly by some big dance halls where a professional dancer could be hired for the duration of a dance.

Although those thirties gramophones and records were so different from those of today, there was on radio a character you would certainly recognise, though his style was very different! He was Christopher Stone, the first disc jockey, and his popularity shows how important radio had become, from the early "cat's whisker" and crystal sets, to nationwide broadcasting at the end of the thirties.

The Radio Years

Sir John Reith, Director General of the BBC speaking at a conference on "Good and Bad Wireless Reception" at the London School of Economics in 1932. You can see some of the sound equipment that was used in the early 1930s at the front of the platform

Switching on the radio is as familiar to us as turning on a tap for a drink of water. And yet for nearly twenty years of the period we are looking at, radio as we know it had not been invented.

The Marconi Company experimented with wireless (as it was always called then) and in 1919 was allowed for the first time to broadcast speech and music from Chelmsford in Essex. These were only experimental transmissions, but in the following year the Daily Mail with the Marconi Company promoted a concert given by Dame Nellie Melba—a famous and buxom singer, whose voice was heard on the air as far away as Newfoundland.

Then, guess what happened? You should be beginning to suspect that whatever was new, and what looked like being fun, would be disapproved of by someone. And someone with authority did disapprove, saying that wireless music was frivolous, and that it might interfere with aircraft communication. So that was that, and in November 1920 the Marconi licence to broadcast was cancelled.

However, wireless broadcasting was too exciting as an idea to be suppressed for long, and in 1922 there were two small broadcasting stations at work, one at Writtle, and the other, the famous 2LO, on top of Marconi House in the Strand, London.

At first, the people who listened to these broadcasts on primitive cats' whisker and crystal sets were members of keen amateur wireless societies, but soon everyone was interested, and the GPO (General Post Office, who issued licences to broadcast) decided it was time to set up a national broadcasting service. And so the British Broadcasting Company (later Corporation) was established, taking over the pioneering 2LO station from Marconi.

The head of the BBC (British Broadcasting Company) was John Reith, a tall, dour Scot, who left his mark on the BBC so firmly that it still bears traces of his ideas. Reith knew exactly what he wanted the BBC to be, and it wasn't always what the listeners wanted. Reith's motto was "offer the public something better than it now thinks it likes".

Let's look at those early wireless sets, and imagine what it was like listening-in to

A two-coil crystal set from the mid-1920s

An announcer, in evening dress, reading the news. You can see an editor passing him a late news item

broadcasts then.

As with the other technical miracles, such as the cinema and the gramophone, wireless was thought to be real magic. I'm sure if you ask around, there are still many people who do not understand how it works. From nowhere, it seemed, came voices, grand orchestras, plays with sound effects, and commentaries on sporting events as they actually happened. No wonder every household longed for a wireless!

The early sets consisted of a pair of headphones, a battery, and a lump of crystal about the size of a pea which acted as a "detector" of the radio waves. If you lived within a reasonable distance—four to twenty miles—of the transmitter, you could pick up the broadcast. But it wasn't that simple!

A piece of wire, called the cat's whisker, had to be placed on exactly the right spot on the crystal to pick up the sound, and then the slightest bump would disturb the connection and you had to start again. And of course, only one person could listen through each set of headphones.

It sounds laborious and primitive, doesn't it? But the excitement and thrill when the cat's whisker hit on the right spot on the crystal, and sounds that were unbelievable poured into your ears, made it worth all the patience, and squabbles over who should have the earphones, and irritation when Mum banged the kitchen door and lost your contact with a performance of the *Magic Flute* opera coming direct from Covent Garden in London.

There were home-construction kits, as there still are, and instructions for making an adequate receiver were given in the first number of *The Wireless Constructor*, the magazine for the new enthusiasm. There was trouble at first with "oscillation", which was something you were doing wrong with your set which interfered with your neighbour's reception, and with its banshee howls and screams it could cause a lot of ill-feeling. You could even be asked personally over the air to adjust your set to stop the row.

Gradually, headphones gave way to loudspeakers, so whole families could listen together. What, apart from Mozart, did people listen to?

There was John Henry, the very first radio comedian, a hen-pecked Yorkshire husband, whose nagging wife would yell, "John Henry! come here," and he would meekly reply "Coming Blossom", a phrase which entered everyday conversation like so many others to come.

Reith was still keeping a firm hand on the broadcasting output, and nothing vulgar or tasteless was allowed. Everything was performed from a script, which had to be checked before any broadcast.

The Announcer soon appeared, and he was required to dress in an evening suit although only technicians and performers could see him. In spite of his posh clothes, he was expected to do all sorts of odd jobs like banging a set of tubular bells which acted as a time signal, shifting furniture, guiding performers through the snaking wires of the studio, and warning them not to sneeze!

There were many and varied broadcasts, sometimes done only because the wireless technicians were amazed at their own, and their medium's, ability to be so clever—so they were sometimes more amazing than interesting. But wireless was still such a novelty to all its listeners that very little seemed boring.

Outside broadcasts like the Armistice Day Ceremony from the Cenotaph in London, and an Evensong service from church, or a commentary on a horse race, were amazingly clever and popular.

An outside broadcast from the Rifle Championships at Bisley, 1928. They were actually broadcasting from the roof of a BBC van!

And we must not forget our first disc jockey, though of course he was not called that then. Christopher Stone conducted a gramophone record request programme in the twenties which was a huge success. People wrote in with their requests, which were very varied and consisted of the music of the day, the foxtrots, slow waltzes and tangos, as well as classical snippets and tunes played on those fantastic cinema organs. Christopher Stone, in his friendly and rather schoolmasterly way, played each one as if it were his personal favourite too.

The dance bands, as we know, were very important in broadcasting, especially in the thirties. If a broadcast was planned from, say, the Carlton Hotel, a microphone was hung over, and in front of, the band, the technicians would telephone the studio to say all was ready, and off they would go. These outside broadcasts were very popular, because not only the music came through the loudspeaker into your sitting-room, but with it the atmosphere of a smart London hotel; the laughter and coughing, the chink of glasses and cutlery, the sound of dancing feet and the applause at the end of each number—shut your eyes and you could be there.

The success which broadcasting brought to those dance bands of the thirties made many of them quick to jump at the idea of ninety minutes' free publicity at the end of the BBC's broadcasting evening. This was a regular pattern in the twenties. Song-plugging (mentioning on the wireless the names of performers and their records) was a problem then, as it is now, and it was so severely disapproved of, that for a short time the BBC forbade all song titles to be named, except those of their own Jack Payne's band.

Jack Payne was so popular that in one year he notched up 650 hours of broadcasting! Autograph hunters hung about Savoy Hill (where the BBC then was) and his annual fan mail amounted to 50,000 letters and postcards. The popularity Jack Payne gained from radio encouraged him to leave the BBC and to increase his fortune touring round variety halls with a band show.

A band leader called Henry Hall replaced Jack Payne at the BBC, and *Henry Hall's Guest Night* was a brilliant idea of his own, and ran for seventeen years. He had a most unprofessional, shy-sounding voice, and he would stumble over his introductions, but he was much loved. He had a knack for picking winners like "The Teddy Bears' Picnic", and when he went on a tour of the Music Halls with his band, all the tickets were sold for every show. Think how much quicker it now was to make yourself known as a show business performer on the wireless, than it had been for those old Music Hall stars, who had to rely on the sale of sheet music, the odd poster, and a whistling errand boy.

As radio producers gained experience and audiences grew larger, the programmes became more ambitious. There were radio plays with strange sound effects and drama serials based on classic novels, and the first "Soap Opera" emerged (soap opera is a continuing serial which can run for years, like *The Archers* on radio today, or *Coronation Street* on television). It was called *The English Family Robinson*, and solemn drama producers frowned upon it; but soon there were others, and they were so successful that listeners wouldn't miss the latest instalment for anything.

BBC scrapbook programmes were also most entertaining, and of course we have them still. Snippets of poetry, prose, music, people remembering the past, all kinds of oddments which appealed to a family group consisting of all ages and sorts of listeners.

Variety on radio, the equivalent of Music Hall on the stage, was slow in gaining ground. The theatre businessmen did not specially want radio to take away their artists. They thought, and perhaps sensibly, that if people could listen in their own homes for next-to-nothing (radio licences were very cheap) to the stars of the Music Hall, they would cease to go to the real thing. So the BBC had its own little concert party in imitation of the stage groups (like the Co-optimists) and called it Radio Radiance. This included in 1926 the comedian Tommy Handley, and—incredibly —a troupe of six tap-dancers who appeared

Henry Hall conducting the BBC Dance Orchestra

before the microphone in full dancing gear. It did not apparently occur to anyone that since all the audience could hear was a rhythmic tapping, dressing up was rather unnecessary.

Then the theatre managements relented and the BBC took the microphone to existing Music Halls, until it created its own in a warehouse on the South Bank of the Thames near Waterloo Bridge in London. This show, *Music Hall*, lasted for twenty years, and was the first programme to have a studio audience, that mixed blessing of instant laughter and applause that we are so used to now.

One of the writer's first radio memories is of a programme called *In Town Tonight*, which was broadcast every Saturday night at 6.30, and which was a regular favourite of most families. I can still hear the opening sounds of rumbling traffic and honking horns, and shouting voices, then the sudden giant voice

shouting "STOP!", followed by an ultra-civilised BBC voice saying "and so once more we stop the mighty roar of London's traffic to bring you interesting people who are *In Town Tonight*".

In 1938, radio produced something very new and only possible on radio, a show called *Band Waggon*. It starred Arthur Askey and Richard Murdoch, and created a total fantasy world, revolving round "a flat at the top of the BBC". (Broadcasting House, standing impressively in Portland Place in London, where it is today, had opened in 1932.)

In this mythical flat, Askey and Murdoch (whom you can see on page 69) regularly met and exchanged conversations and quick-fire jokes with characters like Mrs Bagwash and her daughter Nausea, and since the Askey/Murdoch pair were supposed to be caretakers of the time-signal pips, you can see this was a brand-new kind of humour which was very special to radio.

Foreign broadcasting stations began to loom competitively in the thirties, and it was this competition from Radio Luxembourg, or Radio Normandie, which was listened to by great numbers on Sundays—when Lord Reith's BBC Sunday was still solemn, religious and improving—which forced a change of BBC policy.

Sunday did not altogether lose its dignity and "day of rest" atmosphere, but just before the Second World War, at the end of our period, you could have heard light music, gramophone records, Troise and His Mandoliers, and a talk on gardening, as well as a religious service.

A great many people nowadays use the radio for one thing—the news. Oddly enough, in the early days, newspapers objected strongly to news being broadcast, on the same grounds as the theatre managers objected to the cinema: it would be bad for their business.

By 1934, News ceased to be part of the BBC Talks Department and became an independent department on its own, and the BBC News became *the* authority on world events.

In 1936, one of the most famous personalities of radio reporting had a lucky break. On the night of 30 November 1936, the Crystal Palace, which was a huge glass exhibition centre on a site in Sydenham, caught fire. A young news reporter called Richard Dimbleby (whose first radio interview had been with a record milk-yielding cow called Cherry, who obligingly mooed into the microphone) was sent down to cover the fire. The story was too late for the newspapers,

Sid Walker doing an interview for "In Town Tonight". You can see the sound recordist wearing a pair of headphones

The Crystal Palace on fire—can you imagine Richard Dimbleby trying to broadcast from here? Notice the placards advertising the next show which was to have been held there

and Dimbleby broadcast direct to the nation through a wired-up telephone, with the sounds of fire-engine bells, shouting crowds, and the crackle of the famous Crystal Palace burning down around him. That was news reporting as we know it. The late Richard Dimbleby had two sons, David and Jonathan, whose faces are now as familiar on television as their father's voice became on radio.

One of the most successful radio programmes was *Children's Hour*, and you can read about this in the next chapter.

Television broadcasting began in 1936. It was to become the most dominating of all popular entertainments and after the Second World War pushed radio into second place.

Experiments by Logie Baird and others with small screen transmission had been developed to a good enough standard by 1936 for the BBC to launch a public service of television broadcasting. But in 1939, when the Second World War broke out, television plans

Richard Murdoch (left) and Arthur Askey in "Band Waggon"

were put aside until 1945, leaving twenty thousand viewers who had bought sets with no television to watch. This is not many by today's figures, but it was enough to show that television was popular and would be worth further development.

The price of television sets, at first very expensive, had come down by 1939 to £21 for a table model with a 4 in × 3$\frac{3}{8}$ in screen (truly that small!) and for the better-off a cabinet model, with a 22 in × 18 in screen, was available at £200. Many people bought their sets on weekly instalment plans, and were seeing wonders transmitted from Alexandra Palace in London, such as the Coronation of King George VI and Queen Elizabeth, the historic return of Prime Minister Neville Chamberlain from his meeting with Adolf Hitler in Munich, and many outside events such as

A lady demonstrating a radio and television set at Olympia in August, 1938

A family in a remote country district receiving the news bulletins about the health of King George V in January, 1936

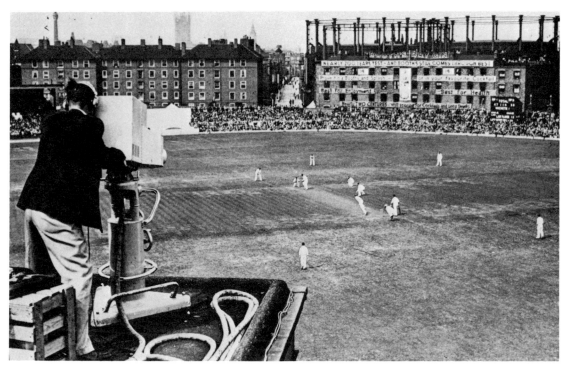

A television outside broadcast of a Test Match at the Oval in August, 1938. Look at the cameraman's seat!

Wimbledon Tennis, Test Match Cricket, Cup Final Football matches, big Boxing matches, and so on.

Plays were also being produced on television. There were in fact 326 plays in those three years. There were magazine programmes like *Picture Page*, and personalities like artist John Piper and gardener Mr Middleton talked about their work. There is an historic television recording of the writer George Bernard Shaw.

Ideas for most programmes of the type we see today had been tried in some form before the screen went blank in September 1939, and it is strange to realise how far back some of today's programme ideas started. As we all know, television came to life again, but that was after 1945, and it is another story.

Specially For Children

A scene from "Peter Pan" at the Duke of York Theatre, London, in 1904

You are probably fed up with being told how spoilt children are today, how you have too much pocket money and how in years gone by children made their own entertainment, didn't have their own television programmes or films, or many books or plays.

It's only recently that children have been thought of as a separate "audience". In the early 1900s, most entertainment was for grown-ups, with children as hangers-on, or as bystanders who didn't always understand or enjoy popular entertainment.

Although *Peter Pan*, the story by J. M. Barrie about a boy who doesn't want to grow up, was first staged in 1904 (and is still a favourite Christmas show) probably radio and cinema were the first entertainments to appreciate that children were not just miniature adults, but had their own sense of humour, liked different kinds of stories, and just didn't understand half the time what grown-ups were on about. Love—depending on what age you were—was either extremely boring or very embarrassing. Jokes about drink and nagging wives, and being short of money, seemed to make Mum and Dad laugh, but children couldn't really see the point.

Adventure stories in books were available for those who could afford to buy them, and there had been "improving" books for children for many years mostly published by the religious societies. But regular popular entertainment for children, not just special events at Christmas or birthday treats, was not part of everyday life in the early part of the 1900s.

Children's tastes change, as the world around them changes, and it may be an eye-opener for you to hear what a theatre critic wrote about the first performance of *Peter Pan* at the Duke of York's Theatre on 27 December 1904. He described how Mr Barrie had concocted a tale of make-believe, which he thought was just what children liked. Pirates, Red Indians, wolves and crocodiles—yes, perhaps you would like those too, but how about "when the first baby laughed, that laugh broke into a thousand pieces, and every piece became a fairy and whenever a child says, 'I don't believe in fairies', a fairy falls down dead"?

The critic thought all this charming and not at all over-sentimental and he, and presumably the delighted audience he described, seemed to find nothing odd about a boy who "ran away to the fairies rather than grow up to be a man".

Even this critic, who loved *Peter Pan*, admitted that "some points of Mr Barrie's

A school outing by waggonette in 1912

This photograph taken in July 1918 shows a tall "Charlie Chaplin" advertising a Charlie Chaplin film

humour will be doubtless lost upon the younger members of his audience", yet *Peter Pan* was written as a play for children and was a huge success.

Peter Pan was not the only play for children, and of course children were entertained in other ways before cinema and radio came. Much of this was organised by groups of Church and Chapel workers, Girl Guides and Boy Scouts. Outings like a summer treat to the seaside and Sunday School concerts were looked forward to all year. "Tea and Entertainment" was a twice- or three-times-a-year event at a church in Northampton, when up to 350 people sat down to a sumptuous tea, and afterwards were entertained by songs and instrumental solos. Children were given Christmas parties, and in the summer there were trips in waggonettes to some pleasant spot for a picnic and games.

However, the entertainment business, run by people who make money out of entertaining thousands of other people, did not think of children as a separate "market" until cinema and radio producers saw the possibilities. Film companies realised that children could be a separate audience.

By the thirties, there was a British Board of Film Censors, which gave certificates to films in much the same way as it does now, sorting out which films are suitable for children on their own, which for children with grown-ups, and which for grown-ups only.

By now there were special film shows for children on Saturday mornings all over the country. These were often second-rate films (perhaps an old Western was included) which were not too frightening or "unsuitable". The way the cinema managers ran these Saturday morning children's performances varied from cinema to cinema.

At some cinemas when the doors opened, a rush would begin and after a certain number had charged down into their seats for tuppence (the "tuppenny rush"), a rope was dropped across the auditorium and the unlucky children behind it had to pay fourpence. The luckier ones with sixpence to spend could stroll in and be sure of a seat in the back row.

Other cinemas had different systems. At one, children would queue for two hours, in the rain and cold if necessary, to be one of the first 200 into the cinema when the doors opened. No rush here—the queue had to move in an orderly fashion past a man sitting at a table, and he would mark a cross on a card which each child kept from week to week. The first 200 were in for tuppence, and if you got fifty-two crosses in a year and that meant going every single week, you were allowed to go to a free Christmas party and cinema show. It is difficult to imagine that the managers were very much concerned about the welfare of the children. In some smart picture palaces, children had to go in by the side door for fear of messing up the shining foyer. And if you think about it, that "free" Christmas party wasn't such a treat when you'd paid fifty-two tuppences over the year for shows which cost the management next to nothing.

Children's cinema did improve. The big circuits (chains of cinemas all owned by one company) and some of the better family-run cinemas were running clubs in quite a different way.

In 1934, the Mickey Mouse Clubs became popular and by 1937 there were 200 of them in Britain. Mickey Mouse is a familiar cartoon character now and he was always a great favourite with children. At the Mickey Mouse Club meetings members really got their money's worth. They had a feature film, or what we know as "the big picture", which was a regular, and was reasonably exciting and

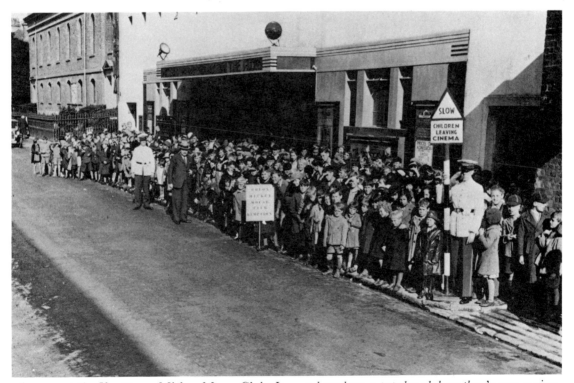

A queue at the Kemptown Mickey Mouse Club. It must have been a popular club as there's even a sign saying "Slow, Children leaving Cinema"

A captivated audience at a children's matinee

interesting for children. Then, of course there were cartoons: Mickey Mouse, Donald Duck and company. These could be followed by live entertainment, such as a magician or juggler, and someone would come along and give an "improving" talk to the children in the audience; for instance a policeman might stand up in front of the screen and give advice on road safety and sensible bicycling habits.

In 1935, Jubilee year for King George V and Queen Mary, the Camberley Mickey Mouse Club opened. Camberley was an army town and specially patriotic, and the Mickey Mouse Club children sent a loyal greeting to their King. They were delighted when his telegram of good wishes in reply was read out at an official opening performance in the cinema. A club song composed by the cinema manager was sung with great gusto, and the audience included the entire Town Council.

Granada Cinemas started Granadier Clubs for children; parents approved and their children became regular film fans. There were comics about cinema heroes like Mickey Mouse and Popeye, and the Clubs continued to mix entertainment and enjoyment with what you might think of as "goody-goody" advice. Members were encouraged to be clean, tidy and neat, generous to those less fortunate than themselves and to be patient in the cinema queue! Thinking back to the rough old days of the "tuppenny rush", the hardship of the war, and back further to the boozy days of the Music Hall, it is not surprising that advice which would improve general standards was willingly accepted, at least by parents!

Praiseworthy as these children's cinema clubs were, the film-makers and cinema managers were businessmen, and a cinema full of ticket-paying children, during a morning when few grown-ups could be expected to attend, was better value than having an empty cinema. Children grow up into adults, and if they already have a weekly cinema-going habit, so much the better for the cinema industry.

From the beginning of radio broadcasting there was radio specially for children. On 23 December 1922, one month after the BBC began its service, there was a daily *Children's Hour*.

The forceful Mr Reith, who later became Lord Reith, said exactly what he wanted *Children's Hour* to be. It was to "provide an hour of clean, wholesome humour, some light music and a judicious sprinkling of information attractively conveyed".

In other words—good clean fun for the kiddies, and if a little education rubbed off on them, well and good.

Once again, remember that tastes change,

and what may seem childish and sentimental to you now, was real magic and wonderfully exciting to young people who had not been entertained as you are today, by television since you could see, or Radio 1 since you could hear.

Children's Hour lasted, in fact, forty-five minutes, and was conducted in the early days by a host of Uncles and Aunties. These were not "presenters" hired specially for the job, but people who were working on the programme anyway. There was Uncle Arthur, Uncle Rex (Arthur Burrows and Rex Palmer) and Uncle Humpty-Dumpty, who was director of the Manchester Station. Uncle Humpty-Dumpty was a strange figure, wrapped in cotton wool, who sat on a stool in front of the microphone and every time he was in danger of falling off, an elephant steadied him, and he carried on.

Now, did you think "how did they get an elephant into the studio?" Well, if you *did*,

Conducting an interview for "Children's Hour!"

you were thinking of television and not radio. There was no need for an elephant, or cotton wool for that matter, all you needed was a convincing Uncle's voice, willing ears and imaginations all over the country.

That was the whole point of radio, and this is why, when John Reith said somewhat pompously "To these children, therefore, the *Children's Hour* must come as a wonderment, truly a voice from another world", he was right.

One of the best examples of radio's use of children's imaginations was a programme which started in the BBC's Northern Region: *Out with Romany.*

Romany was a gypsy character, who with his spaniel dog Raq and two children, went for walks in the countryside and "watched" what was going on. They saw and heard birds, animals and people, witnessed rare sights like otters playing, and heard the reassuring clip-clop of Romany's horse as it slowly pulled along the gypsy caravan.

The truth is, or was, that Romany was the Reverend Bramwell Evens, whose grandfather had been a true gypsy, the two children were two of the Aunties, Muriel (Levy) and Doris (Gambell), who were good at the difficult job of imitating children's voices, and there was no dog, no otter, no birds, no horse and no caravan.

The Reverend Bramwell Evens, or Romany, stood in front of the microphone (though it was his habit to wander off whilst talking, and he did have to be hauled back) and communicated his own real love and enthusiasm for the countryside to an eagerly waiting audience.

As for the rest, the dog, birds, etc., two special effects men, Terry Cox and Jack Hollingsworth, provided barking, and the horse's hooves, and anything else that came in the programme. As Romany didn't always stick to his script, they had to be alert and ready for anything!

When Romany died, in 1943, he was deeply missed, and children wrote in to the BBC saying so, and worrying about what would happen to the dog Raq—would he be left alone in the caravan?

As well as *Out With Romany*, there were other favourites: *The Zoo Man*, stories of Worzel Gummidge, plays and serials, sometimes adapted from books by well-known children's writers, sometimes specially written for *Children's Hour*.

And there was *Toy Town*; this was an imaginary world of toys and people with names like Larry the Lamb, Mr Inventor, Dennis the Dachshund, and Mr Mayor-sir. It was rather like the cartoons on television for very small children, and had the same charm and humour. But, of course, there were no pictures, these were in the listeners' heads.

Children's Hour was so real, with its Uncles and Aunties, that children would write in and become "members" with badges to prove it. The BBC organised "personal appearances" by the Uncles and Aunties, and one with the unlikely name of Uncle Caractacus claims to have kissed 800 Birmingham children in an hour. Ugh!—kissed? It's that sentimental approach again, and another example of how tastes have changed. The children didn't mind being kissed, nor being called girlies, babies and kiddies. It was all quite natural to them then.

In the early days, all letters were replied to on the programme, but eventually there were too many coming in, and only birthdays or sick children got a mention. Occasionally, parents would write in for a birthday child, and ask the Uncle to give clues as to where a present was hidden in the child's living-room. Then with directions from the wireless, the child would find his hidden treat. That must have made *Children's Hour* seem real indeed.

Another funny phrase which shows how times have changed was Uncle Caractacus' "signing-off" message. He would always say goodbye by wishing children pleasant dreams and a nice hot bath!

This got him into a bit of trouble, as it was pointed out that a good half of the children listening were too poor to have a bath anyway. But he carried on, thinking maybe of Reith's belief that *Children's Hour* would be just on the level of the English solid middle

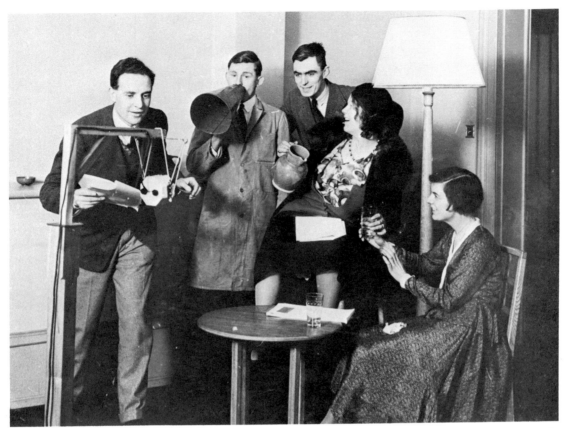

Here the cast are recording Miss Rhoda Power's History Lesson. The special effects man is ready to make his contribution

class, and those beneath would be uplifted by listening in, and might even be encouraged to try and improve their rotten living conditions.

Children's Hour lasted until 1964, and many people wish it would return. But would you listen to it now? Could it compete with *Magpie* and *Blue Peter* on television? Have you got the same active imagination as those children in 1922?

We said earlier that cinema businessmen could see good financial sense in having cinema especially for children. But what about radio? What profit could be made out of children here?

Remember that in 1922, it was the British Broadcasting Company (not Corporation), and this company was made up of a number of manufacturers of wireless sets. They had put money into setting up a radio system, and

their return would be in the number of sets sold. So now you see that just as you might pester your parents for a colour television, so those children in the twenties might persist "We want a wireless, so we can hear *Children's Hour*, like the kids next door." And that was another set sold.

In the 1930s the most famous of the commercial radio stations, Radio Luxembourg, had the idea of selling their sponsor's product—Ovaltine—through child listeners. A group of children, called the "Ovaltineys", sang a jingle which some people will still remember:

We are the Ovaltineys,
Little girls and boys . . .

The song went on to show how happy and healthy you could be if you drank Ovaltine!

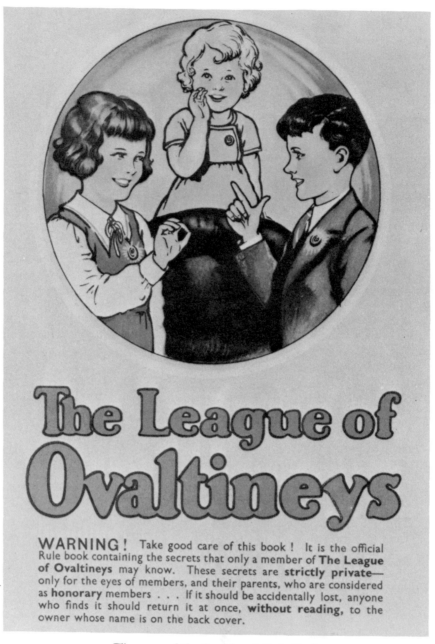

The cover of the Ovaltineys' Rule Book

There were Ovaltiney badges and an Ovaltiney club. There was another group called the Cococubs (Cadbury's) and both they and their rival Ovaltineys recorded their songs at the same London studio and left messages for each other scrawled in lipstick on the dressing-room mirrors. The Ovaltineys became a radio craze which no doubt sold many a tin of Ovaltine while it lasted.

By 1939, then, children as a separate audience were generally accepted, and there were films, radio programmes and gramophone records (some using those BBC Uncles and Aunties) for them alone.

Fair's Coming!

A traditional form of popular entertainment, which every one of you must at some time have visited, is the Fair. There have been fairs for hundreds of years, and a town fair today, such as Banbury Fair, occupying the whole centre of the town, is as exciting to you now as it was to children in the first forty years of our century.

But for adults and children in country districts and even small towns who were not accustomed to any other form of entertainment, except what local talent could produce, the coming of the Fair was a great event, looked forward to all the year round.

The fair was for everybody. If you were reasonably well off, there was plenty to spend your money on. If you were poor, and a great many were, then you could have perhaps one go on an Aunt Sally to try to win a prize, and then spend the rest of the evening wandering about watching others spending their money, and keeping your eyes down some of the time in case coins had been dropped in the gutter, or on the grass of the village green.

The annual visit of the fair remains very clear in the minds of many elderly people.

I remember the fair always came in the school holidays [says a Northamptonshire lady in her middle sixties]. It was to celebrate the church's feast day—St Lawrence, it was, and his day is 22nd August. So the fair came to our town on the weekend after that, if the 22nd fell during the week.

They came in motorised caravans, and the children would run to meet them. A shout had gone round: "Fair's coming," and we'd all chase off down the road to see what was coming that year. They had it emblazoned on the sides of their vans, you see, Thurston's roundabouts, swing-boats and gondolas etc., and there were some real old gypsy caravans too.

They set up the fair in our market place. It was in two halves with a tall Coronation pole in the centre, and seats round it. A road went through the middle, and that sort of divided the fair in half. We used to watch them setting up the roundabouts, and the horses ... oh, the horses were our favourites! Folks called Billings had the horses' roundabout, it had an organ in the middle playing really well, and we always thought the Billings were a cut above the rest of the fair people.

My father used to warn us about not going too near the caravans, some of the men looked rather rough, but I don't suppose they'd have done us any harm. But that was part of the excitement, especially after dark, when they lit the naphtha flares and everywhere was flickering shadows.

Of course, all the roundabouts, even the organ on the horses, were steam-driven. They had those great steam engines like steam-rollers, to give the power, and the noise was terrific. It was the noise and the wavering lights at night I liked best.

It was a great day. For the Feast dinner on the Sunday, we had roast duck and baked plum pudding. But Saturday was the day for the fair, and all the farmers and all our relations would come in from the country. It was a great get-together, and if you were lucky, you'd get extra goes on things, your uncles and aunties would treat you—"Here, have another go on the horses," they'd say.

The Fair at Northampton. Can you spot the roundabout belonging to the Billings family?

There were hoop-la's and darts, rifle ranges and coconut shies, as well as swing-boats and gondolas, and then there were things to eat, toffee and brandy-snaps. I used to love brandy-snaps! Rock, they had, like seaside rock. My mother wouldn't let us have toffee apples, she said you never knew where they were made, though I don't know why that didn't apply to the other things!

The fair got going soon after tea. Little children would stand around, and when the fair people started to get ready, a shout would go round the town: "Canvas off!" This meant the huge canvas cover which protected the beautiful horses on the roundabout was being taken off and everything was about to open up. We'd rush down, clutching our few pence, because times were hard, you know, and we had to select carefully what we wanted to go on. You had to make your money last.

I had to be home by dark, if I was on my own, but could stay later with my mother and father. Some poorer children just lived round the fair for the whole week it was there. The fair women were quite kind, but they looked different from us and so did the children. Their faces were tanned, from always being out of doors, and often their hair was long and greasy. That was unusual in those days! I think the strangeness made it more exciting. And I used to love to watch the way the fair women and men could really make people spend their money. They were so clever at persuading them. Sometimes people won prizes on the rifle range and darts—cheap gaudy dolls, and garish coloured ornaments.

There was no strong drink at the fair, but of course there were pubs all round where the men went for their beer.

Everyone loved the fair, except perhaps the people who lived over the shops round the market place. It must have been difficult trying to get to sleep in fair week!

That lady remembered so much about the fair, it is easy to see that it was the high spot of her year, as far as popular entertainment went.

The other travelling entertainment was, of course, the circus. The big ones would set up at Wembley and other permanent sites in big towns for several winter weeks, including Christmas and New Year, and then they would pack their huge trailers and go out "on the road".

A visit to the circus was a regular Christmas treat for many children, and the big ring with its Ringmaster and clowns, high-wire walkers, trapeze artists, acrobats, jugglers and bare-back riders, was a thrilling spectacle. Then there were the "wild" animals, some so obviously tame that the so-called dangerous feats they would perform with their masters were true show-business illusion. But occasionally a lion-tamer would be mauled by a bad-tempered lioness, and an elephant could get bored with the same old tricks and decide to run amok.

Circus entertainment was a little like the fair, in the way that its people were separate from the everyday folk they entertained. Circus people especially had, and still have, a highly organised world of their own, and their way of life, which is mostly travelling, but which works up to the big winter season, is one which is passed down through generations of the same families.

Just after the First World War, the circus had a very bad time. Most of the men had gone off to be soldiers and many were killed. And the circus horses, too, had been taken—maybe you wouldn't think of that, but huge numbers of horses were used to pull guns and transport stores and men in the war. Other forms of popular entertainment, like revue and musical comedy, variety and the early films, were flourishing and took customers away from circuses, and it was many years before the great circuses like Bertram Mills' built themselves up again.

Both the circus and the fair were once-a-year entertainments, and of course there were many more of these which large numbers of people enjoyed. In the late twenties, the Ideal Home Exhibition drew huge crowds to London, just as it does now; there were Football Cup Finals, Boat Race Days, the Chelsea Flower Show, the Royal Tournament, the Hendon Air Display, and Sir Alan Cobham's Air Circus which toured round like an ordinary circus. There was Wimbledon

All the fun of the fair at Barnet in 1919

The Wallendas performing their high-wire act at Olympia in 1932

A stand at the Ideal Home Exhibition at Olympia in 1928

Tennis and the Crufts Dog Show, the Grand National race at Aintree and Derby Day at Epsom, which included a really splendid fair.

A season of opera at Covent Garden was part of the London scene, and out in the suburbs men and women went greyhound racing, a new entertainment which began in 1927. There was motor racing at Brooklands, and dirt-track racing and all kinds of ways of entertaining yourself at home, the piano still being a favourite in most families.

Music Hall, cinema, theatre, dancing, radio and gramophone were the most popular entertainments, and when people wanted a night out, the pictures, the theatre and Palais de Danse were where most of them went.

A Night Out

We began with a night out at the Music Hall, and the story ends with three different ways of being entertained in the 1930s.

. . . at the Cinema

Try to imagine the Princess Cinema in a small town in the north of England where Britain's first full-length talkie, *Blackmail*, is showing this week, in the early thirties.

Old Mrs Higginbotham had arrived. She was puffing and panting a bit from the three long, straight streets between her small, damp and dark terraced house, 59 Balmoral Road, and the Princess Cinema in the Market Square, opposite the grimy-looking Town Hall and Council Offices.

Mrs Higginbotham paused, leaning on her stick and looked up to the board above the front archway of the cinema. She read, "*Blackmail*, Britain's First Full-Length Talking Moving Picture." She had seen American talkies once or twice as she was a regular at the Princess, but now here was one made in Britain by . . . she peered up again . . . Alfred Hitchcock, and not a silent movie hastily adapted to sound in the last few reels of film, like many had been, but talking all the way through!

The wind blew gustily round the Market Square and Mrs Higginbotham pulled her late husband's grey check scarf tight round her neck. She stepped up the two shallow steps between black "marble" columns supporting elaborate carved stone and a frieze of grapes and leaves over the top, through the open glass-paned doors and into the foyer. It had a warm red carpet and photographs of Douglas Fairbanks, Mary Pickford and Anna May Wong, who with her wide Chinese features and her graceful oriental dances was a favourite with Mrs Higginbotham.

Mrs Bryant was in the ticket office as usual, dressed in her neat black silk dress, her hair drawn into a bun at the back of her head. Mrs Bryant was old-fashioned and proud of it, and she and her husband ran the Princess with the help of two daughters, two sons and one son-in-law, together with extra staff drawn from relations and friends. It was a family affair, and the social centre of the town.

As Mrs Higginbotham hobbled up to the ticket office, Mrs Bryant leaned forward to look through the little glass window with its arched cut-out, and smiled.

"Hallo, Ethel love—how are you today?"

"Me legs is bad," replied Mrs Higginbotham, "but that old house is no good fer me. I can't afford but a bit o' coal on Sundays, and the damp's creeping up the walls like bedbugs!"

Mrs Bryant shivered. "Well, you're in fer a treat tonight, Ethel love," she said consolingly, "this *Blackmail* is best we've 'ad. Take yer right out of yerself, it will. You can 'ave yer money back if it doesn't."

Mrs Higginbotham handed her ninepence (carefully saved up in a little china pot on her mantelpiece at home) over the counter to Mrs Bryant. She was given an orange ticket, and with a cheery, "You're in plenty of time, Ethel

love, queue's not started yet," from Mrs Bryant, the old lady made her way into the lighted cinema.

Mary Bryant, the youngest daughter, stood inside the swing door, neat and welcoming in her black dress, a brooch pinned to the white collar, and her white apron starched and ironed to perfection. She held out her hand for Mrs Higginbotham's ticket (a formality, because she knew Mrs Higginbotham very well indeed, and was perfectly certain she would never try to get in without paying) and as she was taking the old lady's arm to guide her to her usual seat beside the warm radiator, three small and ragged boys sidled past. "Here," said Mary, "tickets please!"

The boys stopped, looking miserable. Two of them were about the same size, the third quite a lot smaller. Two hands held out two tickets, and the trio began to move away, the little one hidden behind the other two. "What about 'im!" said Mary sharply.

They stopped again, and after a short silence, the biggest boy said " 'e ain't got one,

Miss." Mrs Higginbotham stood waiting, enjoying this unexpected piece of drama.

"Get along then," said Mary, after a short hesitation, "get into tha' seats before I notice 'im."

And she turned back to Mrs Higginbotham, as they scuttled down the aisle into seats in the shadows. "Them's the Blackburn kids," she said, "no good sendin' 'em 'ome, there won't be Mother nor Father there. They're better off 'ere in the warm." She put her hand under Mrs Higginbotham's arm and helped her carefully into her place, holding down the tip-up seat so the old lady could settle herself comfortably.

Mrs Higginbotham looked round, and waved to a couple of friends two rows behind, and to Mr Pomfrey whose gammy leg stuck out into the aisle and tripped people up in the dark.

The cinema was beginning to fill up now (the queue always stretched right round two sides of the market square on a Saturday night) and soon the lights went down. The screen curtains parted—shimmering, silvery ripples over the first advertising slide for Horton's Drapers in Market Street.

There were several of these slides, all for local shops and suppliers:

For a Good Article at a Low Price
GO TO
R. E. SMITH'S
Practical Tailor, Hood Street

and

Where do you get the best Milk?
Why, from Newtown
Who supplies it?
W. J. ROBERTS
West Street.
Fresh Butter and Eggs

This last advertisement always made old Mrs Higginbotham's mouth water. She could scarcely afford the bread, let alone fresh butter and eggs.

"Mm," she thought to herself, "I suppose the ninepence I paid to come here would have bought me some butter."

But the warmth, the friendly atmosphere and the films, which took her far away from dingy Balmoral Road, were worth far more to her than ninepennyworth of butter.

After the advertisements came a travelogue. This was a film about Lake Geneva in Switzerland and Mrs Higginbotham watched the boats and climbers on the Alps, and the sun shining and shining. She was back in her youth when she and Mr Higginbotham went on a three-day holiday to the Lake District and she had twisted her ankle, and he'd said . . . but now the newsreel was starting.

The newsreels fascinated Mrs Higginbotham. She always thought one day she might see someone she knew, and scanned closely the crowd scenes at the Derby, or the Boat Race, or processions of the Royal Family. So far, all the faces were strange ones, but she truly believed one day she might see Cousin Alice who lived in London, standing there on the pavement waving to the King.

Then came a trailer for next week's film but Mrs Higginbotham missed that bit, as she was craning her neck to look round at a disturbance in the back of the cinema. Some big lads were lurching about, voices raised and fists flying. William Bryant, the eldest son, and his brother-in-law, George Jackson, a big tough lad himself, appeared, and in no time the unruly group had been removed, and Mrs Higginbotham returned to the screen. The titles were coming up for *Blackmail*, so she tucked her feet under the radiator, and prepared to be amazed, entertained, thrilled and, if necessary, terrified!

Mrs Higginbotham was not disappointed. The hero was played by one of her favourite actors, John Longden, and the heroine by a Czechoslovakian girl called Anny Ondra (what Mrs Higginbotham didn't know was that Anny's accent was much too thick for a talkie, and another actress's voice was saying the words while Anny mouthed them).

John Longden was a detective and Anny Ondra, his girlfriend. A murder was committed and Anny Ondra somehow got involved. She was then blackmailed and John Longden had the terribly difficult job of being a police detective and coming to grips with certain evidence that showed his girlfriend could have been the murderer.

Mrs Higginbotham's hands were tightly clasped round her old battered handbag, and she lived every minute of the film as it unwound. At last "The End" came up on the screen, and Mrs Higginbotham struggled to her feet for "God Save the King". She came back to reality slowly, as Mary helped her out of her seat and into the foyer.

"Did you enjoy it, Ethel love?" called Mrs Bryant, from her little office. "My word, I did," said Mrs Higginbotham. "I shall think about that murderer all the way 'ome!"

"You'll be quite safe love, our William'll see yer to the corner."

As she went out into the dark street, the youngest of the Bryants, fourteen-year-old Walter, came chasing after her. "Mrs Higginbotham! Mam forgot to tell you, your Doris called in and left word to say she'd be round tomorrow after all, her Ted's gone back to work."

"Thank God for that!" said Mrs Higginbotham, and hobbled off on William's arm, her stick tapping the pavement and her mind full of Anny Ondra's awful predicament. Just supposing she'd not gone off with that bloke ... "This'll do yer, Mrs Higginbotham," William cut into her thoughts. "See yer next week ... Cheerio!"

... at the Theatre

And now off to the theatre in a big Midland town, where Noel Coward's play, *Private Lives*, is showing.

"Hurry up, m'dear!" shouted John Bickerstaff, from the foot of the stairs. His two children, Douglas and Mary, ready for bed in their pyjamas, peeped down through the bannisters to see their father dressed in his best dark suit, his black hair neatly parted with a shining white line, and flattened with hair cream to fit his head like a sleek swim-cap.

"What time will you be back?" asked Mary. She knew the answer, really, because her parents often went to the New Theatre in town on Saturday evenings, and they always came back at about ten-thirty or eleven o'clock. But she was spinning out the time before being sent to bed. She had heard on Children's Hour, Uncle Caractacus' instructions to have "sweet dreams and a nice hot bath," and her parents always agreed with this sensible routine.

"Same as usual, Mary dear," said her mother, sailing out of her bedroom in a cloud of scent and a trailing fox fur tippet. "Mrs Brown will be in to look after you directly."

"It's seven o'clock already!" Father looked ostentatiously at his watch, and unhooked his long, dark overcoat from the hall stand. Mother stopped opposite the mirror and put on her lavender-coloured gloves, which matched her low-waisted crepe dress. She looked admiringly at herself and patted her hair. The pats weren't necessary, it was perfectly waved and curled close to her head, and secured with a little sparkly butterfly on a clip ("only sixpence from Woolworth's," she'd assured her husband).

"Goodbye!" shouted the children in their pyjamas from the bannisters above, "Have a nice time!"

"Thanks, darlings," called Mrs Bickerstaff, tripping neatly past Mr Bickerstaff, who grumpily banged the front door after them. He helped his wife into the front seat of their tiny Austin Seven, and starting the engine at the third try, drove off jerkily down Acacia Avenue.

Parking in a side street behind the theatre, Mr and Mrs Bickerstaff, arm-in-arm, she clutching a flat evening purse and he smiling now that he saw in fact they had plenty of time, walked round the large bulk of the theatre building to the front.

Mrs Bickerstaff always loved this moment. Coming out of the darkness of Norton Alley into the main High Street, she saw once more the brilliant lights of the New Theatre, the stream of people, all in their best clothes just like herself and John, chattering and laughing as they hurried into the theatre.

Taxis were drawing up, and a uniformed commissionaire held open the doors with one hand, while at the same time he held the other palm-upwards in the hope of a tip from the alighting passengers.

On the pavement to one side of the main doors of the theatre was the regular "outside" entertainer—Old Harry, he was called. Not that he was particularly old but he looked so down-at-heel in his long rusty black coat and bent felt hat. On his violin he played sweet, sad tunes which Mrs Bickerstaff recognised as coming from the musical shows of the time. She tossed a threepenny-bit into the faded red velvet lining of his violin case, and read once more the defiant notice, handwritten and propped up against the wall: "Cinema musician put out of work by the talkies—wife and three children to support". "I do wish he wouldn't stand just there," Mrs Bickerstaff whispered to her husband, "he spoils my evening. I can't put him out of my mind."

In the foyer, a crowd of theatre-goers waited until the last moment to go in. A few were smoking cigarettes and some had long black or greenish cigarette-holders in imita-

tion of their favourite stage or film stars. Some people were queueing to leave their coats in the cloakroom to one side of the foyer.

"Have you got the tickets?" asked Mrs Bickerstaff in sudden alarm. Her husband usually picked up their regular six-shilling seats when he finished work at the Bank on Saturday lunchtime. But she always had a dread of him not remembering, and then there'd be no spare seats, and they would have to go home and their lovely warm, exciting evening at the theatre would have come to nothing.

"Don't fuss," said Mr Bickerstaff as usual, "I've got them in my wallet," and he produced them to hand to the uniformed attendant, who thanked him politely and ushered Mr and Mrs Bickerstaff to their seats half-way down the aisle in the stalls.

The New Theatre was not completely new. It had been built to replace an older one about ten years ago; it was warm, comfortable, and in Mrs Bickerstaff's eyes, anyway, very elegant. There were red plush seats with little

brass ashtrays fixed to the back of every other seat, carpeted aisles and cosy-looking boxes at the sides, all looking expectantly towards the stage. Long pink velvet curtains, edged with gold braid and tassels, hung at the front, hiding the stage. Mrs Bickerstaff settled herself in her seat, sent her long-suffering husband back up the aisle to buy a programme and a box of chocolates, and waited happily for her evening's entertainment to begin.

The play was Noel Coward's *Private Lives* and she'd been greatly looking forward to it. Her doctor's wife, whom she'd met at the Church Sale of Work yesterday afternoon, had seen it "ages ago" in London, with Noel Coward himself playing the star part. "Marvellous, Mrs Bickerstaff," the doctor's wife had said, "of course, it won't be quite the same without dear Noel in it, but still, you're sure to enjoy it."

Mr Bickerstaff was back, the rest of the audience settled itself, the lights slowly went down, and the curtains separated.

The scene was set with two adjoining

balconies overlooking a moonlit bay on the south coast of France. Lights of boats were twinkling in the harbour (Mrs Bickerstaff couldn't actually see these, but the two characters on stage kept referring to them). Looking out to sea was an elegant gentleman, whilst his newly-married wife was unpacking in the bedroom behind. She joined her husband after a minute or two to drink a cocktail and exchange witty and romantic conversation.

Then, another elegant newly-married couple appeared, talking not quite so wittily to each other, but revealing that each wife had formerly been married to the other's husband. Mrs Bickerstaff relaxed, discreetly munched two or three chocolates and sighed contentedly.

During the interval, whilst sorting out the tangles of the story for her husband, Mrs Bickerstaff sipped a Moussec at the little bar, crushed amongst all the other members of the audience discussing the play.

"Well, what are these Elyot and Amanda people going to do now they're back together again?" said John Bickerstaff, a little impatient with the to-ings and fro-ings of married people on stage, who seemed to care nothing for the rules of staying married and bringing up a family, by which he lived.

But Mrs Bickerstaff loved it all—"Oh, isn't Amanda lovely!" she said dreamily, "I'm sure they'll stay together in Paris and life will just be one long second honeymoon for them . . ."

She wasn't quite right, but the rest of the play was satisfactorily full of twists and turns, quarrelling and making it up again and a great deal more witty remarks. When she and Mr Bickerstaff emerged from the theatre on to a wet and shiny pavement, she said, "She was right, you know."

"Who?—Amanda?" said Mr Bickerstaff, thinking he'd sorted it all out at last. "No, our doctor's wife, she said we'd enjoy it enormously," replied Mrs Bickerstaff.

"Oh," said Mr Bickerstaff, and turning up his coat collar, he added, "Well, I'm glad you liked it, my dear. Just hang on here a minute,

and I'll pop round and bring the Austin to pick you up."

Mrs Bickerstaff just said, "Mmm," and turned to gaze at the large photographs of the play's stars, looking out so elegantly and uncaringly at the wet town around them.

. . . at the Palais

All dressed up, we go dancing in London, at the Hammersmith Palais.

"Who's at the Palais this week?" Muriel asked her friend Olive, as they climbed into the trolleybus at the end of a not too hard day's work in the office.

Both girls were typists at a firm of accountants in the west London suburb of Shepherd's Bush. They lived in Chiswick and travelled to and fro each day, climbing to the top deck of the smoothly-humming trolleybus, with its overhead power-line stretching down the middle of the street.

The Palais they were discussing was the one on Hammersmith Broadway, generally agreed by the girls to be the best in these last years of the 1930s, and a regular favourite for their Saturday evening outings. They went either with boys they knew or together, hoping to find boyfriends from the enormous crowds which turned up.

"My Dad says he's not too keen on my going every week," said Olive, "but I think he and Mum are a bit old-fashioned. I told them it's very respectable, and nothing bad happens . . ." They looked at each other and giggled. "Well," said Muriel, "no-one gets drunk, do they? Not on Coke and Lemonade!"

"Your stop," said Olive, getting up to let Muriel out of the seat. "See you tomorrow night, then?"

"Righto," shouted Muriel, as she stepped lightly down the trolleybus stairs, "I think Charlie's taking me—but I'll see you there."

Muriel's father also worked in an office. He was a clerk in a London exporting firm in the City, and went to work each day by Underground train. He was small, neat and extremely respectable. Muriel was his only daughter and the apple of his eye. He didn't approve of dancing at the Hammersmith Palais, and he didn't really approve of Charlie. But Muriel could always get round him, and tonight Charlie was expected to call and escort her to the Palais, with a promise to be home by quarter past eleven at the latest.

Muriel had been a long time up in her bedroom, and now she opened the living-room door with a flourish and took a few steps inside, pausing in a posed position, one hand twisting the curl on her right cheek and the other stretched out casually holding a green purse on a long chain.

"Oh crumbs, Dad!" said Muriel's mother sentimentally, "doesn't she look a peach?" Muriel's father grunted, "Mmm, very nice." "D'you like my new dress, Dad? It's the latest thing," said Muriel. She held up the pale green scarf which hung round her neck. It matched her shortish, silky dress, and the material was semi-transparent. Muriel's arms were bare, and as she moved her head, long pale green glass earrings swung to and fro catching the light.

"T'isn't decent if you want to know what I think," said her father, and went back to his greyhound racing results in the evening paper.

A knock at the front door prevented Muriel from replying, and she disappeared to greet Charlie, a smart lad who worked in a store in the Chiswick High Road, selling clothes for men. He was very smartly turned out too, in an outfit from America, sold quite cheaply in his department. His wide trousers and pointed-toe shoes were a chestnut brown, his pullover striped in various shades of fawn, and his jacket was wide-shouldered and rather short.

"Evenin' Guv," he said to Muriel's father, who looked up with a frown and said: "All this gadding about, dressed up to the nines. You never read the papers, I s'pose."

"What do you mean, Guv?" asked Charlie.

"'Aven't you noticed? Trouble's brewin'," the older man replied. "You'll soon 'ave somethin' more serious to think about than dancin' if somebody don't take this Adolf 'itler in 'and."

Mum said: "Oh leave off, Dad. Let 'em enjoy themselves while they can," and Muriel, impatient to be gone, put on her coat, ushered Charlie out and slammed the front door. ("That's their Muriel again," said their next door neighbour, as she felt her house shake, "spoilt brat!")

Charlie and Muriel walked arm-in-arm to the trolleybus stop. "Olive's going tonight," said Muriel, "hope she finds a partner, or we shall be stuck with her."

"Thought she was your friend," said Charlie, as the trolleybus swung round the corner and drew up. "Oh well, if you don't mind . . ." said Muriel with a pout.

Outside the Hammersmith Palais, under the lighted sign, "Joe Loss and His Band", with a brilliant illuminated impression of the band in action, the usual crowd of keen dancers was arriving. A few solitary girls or lads stood waiting anxiously for their partners, among them Olive, who grinned as she recognised Charlie and Muriel.

"Hallo," said Muriel, not very enthusiastically. There were usually more girls than boys at the Palais, and she didn't particularly want to share Charlie with Olive for the evening. Charlie, however, seemed to like the idea of a girl on each arm, and led them across to buy their tickets.

"Let's go dutch," said Olive, "I've still got most of my wages left." There was an awkward pause. Muriel had no money in her little green purse, only a lipstick, powderpuff and comb. The Palais was known to be a place where you held on tightly to your purse, or even left it with old Mrs Burnett in the brightly lit kiosk just off the ballroom. It cost you a penny or two to leave it there but you knew it was safe.

Charlie rose to the occasion with pride. "I'll treat you both, just this once," he said; "got an increase this week, as a matter of fact, so I can afford it."

Olive thanked him effusively and Muriel looked cross. This made them even more of an uncomfortable trio!

Across the carpeted foyer, past the fan-shaped, opaque glass wall-lights, and the photographs of coming attractions at the Palais, Charlie and the girls walked with the streams of dancers into the ballroom. There was always a rather undignified scramble for gilt tables and chairs placed on the carpeted section surrounding the dance floor, and those who couldn't get a seat stood leaning up against the wall, or against one of the pillars which supported a balcony above.

Charlie and Muriel found two seats quickly, and Olive followed more slowly, pausing at Mrs Burnett's kiosk to leave her purse. There was no seat for her when she caught up with her friends and Charlie half-rose to offer her his. "No thanks, Charlie," she said, catching Muriel's thunderous look. "I think I see a girl from the office over there, I want a word with her," and she walked off towards one of the pillars, where a short, curly-haired girl in a blue dress was nonchalantly leaning, trying hard to look as if she didn't mind being on her own.

"Phew!" said Muriel, "that's a lucky thing," and smiled alluringly at Charlie. "I'll have a dance with her later," he said, just a little annoyed with Muriel. "Do you want a drink?"

"Yes please, Coca-Cola as usual," Muriel replied, and gazed round the ballroom as Charlie disappeared.

The band was on a raised dais in the centre of one of the long sides of the ballroom. Behind it was a decorative pattern of zig-zag strip lighting and painted fan-shapes. The band itself was smart and slick in dinner jackets and bow-ties. Joe Loss, the leader, held a little baton and tapped his right foot rhythmically on the dais as he conducted the music. They were playing " 'Twas on the Isle of Capri that I found her," and Muriel hummed the catchy tune softly to herself.

A man loomed up in front of her. He was older than Charlie, and his face looked pale, as if he didn't get enough fresh air. "Would you like to dance?" he said, with a little bow. "Oh lor," said Muriel to herself, "now what do I do?" She was half flattered at being asked to dance by such a sophisticated older man, and half scared in case he was one of those

"nasty types" her father was always going on about.

Then she saw Charlie across the floor, chatting to Olive and the other girl on his way back with the drinks, and she decided. "Thanks," she said, and got up to dance.

They were half-way round the dance floor, when suddenly the music stopped. All the dancers looked towards the band leader, as he turned to make an announcement. It was to be a spot waltz, and Muriel's partner, whose name she had discovered was Roy, clasped her close and held her more tightly. Muriel was a bit alarmed. His hands were clammy, and all the girls said this was a bad sign. She looked round anxiously for Charlie, and to her relief she saw him approaching. He tapped Roy on the shoulder, and "Excuse me," he said firmly. "Buzz off, it's not an 'excuse me' dance," said Roy, turning Muriel deftly away in another direction. "He's a lovely dancer," thought Muriel, in spite of herself.

"Come on, mate, she's with me," said Charlie, following them and beckoning to a big broad-shouldered man standing at the side and looking at them. Roy saw the man take a couple of steps towards them, recognised the Palais "chucker-out" and dropped his arms from Muriel. "Carry on, then," he said nastily, "she's a rotten dancer, anyway."

"Good enough for me," said Charlie smartly, and waltzed Muriel away down the room. The music stopped mid-phrase, and a spot-light roamed around the floor. It picked out Muriel and Charlie, much to Muriel's delight, and as everyone clapped, they went forward to collect a box of chocolates from the dais.

The rest of the evening passed quickly, with a prize for the best tango, a lively session of the Palais Glide to the tune of "Poor Little Angeline" as lines of dancers joined hands and wove patterns of steps across the dance floor, and "Hands-Knees-and-Bumpsa-Daisy" was pretty lively, too.

Muriel stuck to Charlie like glue, Olive was seen dancing a lot with Roy, and then disappeared. "I'll hear all about it at the office," said Muriel, as they danced the last

waltz, with the lights dimmed and all the couples dreamily revolving.

"Eleven o'clock," said Charlie, "time to go." They sat hand-in-hand on the trolleybus in silence. Suddenly Muriel said, "Who d'you think that Roy was?"

"One of those gigolo chaps, I reckon," said Charlie, "you could hire a dancing partner for money—Victor Sylvester started as one of those."

Victor Sylvester's records of strict tempo dance music were favourites of Muriel's, and she and Charlie often did a "slow, slow, quick-quick, slow" foxtrot round the tiny living-room of Muriel's house.

"I thought he was a good dancer," said Muriel, "but he was a bit nasty about me—after all, we did learn proper ballroom dancing at those classes, didn't we?"

"Don't worry," said Charlie, "he was just narked because I butted in. Got to look after you, haven't I?—show your Dad the Palais isn't just a 'pick-up' . . ."

Muriel looked out into the dark streets. "I felt sort of sorry for him though," she said, as they got up at their bus stop. "Still, it'll be something to talk to Olive about on Monday."

Acknowledgments

The author and publishers would like to thank the following for their help in supplying the photographs used in this book and for giving permission for them to be reproduced

BBC Copyright Photographs pp. 63, 66, 69, 70 (bottom), 71, 79.
Alan Burman p. 82.
Miss E. B. Hepworth p. 25.
Metro-Goldwyn-Mayer Pictures Ltd. p. 48.
National Film Archive Stills Library pp. 25, 26, 33, 39, 40, 47, 52, 75.
Radio Times Hulton Picture Library, cover photograph, pp. 2, 8, 10, 11, 22, 24, 27, 29, 34, 35, 37, 41, 44, 46, 51, 53, 54, 55 (left), 57, 58, 60, 61, 62, 64, 67, 68, 70 (top), 73, 74, 76, 77, 84, 86.
The Raymond Mander and Joe Mitchenson Theatre Collection pp. 9, 12, 13, 17, 18, 19, 20, 55 (right), 56, 72, 85.
RKO General Pictures p. 49.
Paramount Pictures Corporation p. 43.
Walt Disney Productions Limited p. 50.
Wander Limited p. 80.

Bibliography

Biggest Aspidistra in the World, Peter Black (BBC).
Music Hall in Britain, D. F. Cheshire (David and Charles).
Picture Palace, Audrey Field (Gentry Books).

The cover photograph shows a scene from a Harold Lloyd film.
The drawings on pp. 88, 91 and 95 are by Anthony Morris.